African American History

A Journey of Liberation

Second Edition

Dr. Molefi Kete Asante

Worktext
Created and Written
by
Charmaine Harris-Stewart
Theresa Flynn-Nason
David J. Glunt

 The Peoples Publishing Group, Inc.

Free to Learn, to Grow, to Change

1-800-822-1080

www.journeyofliberation.com

ISBN 1-56256-603-2

First edition published 1995
Second edition published 2001

Printed in the United States of America
20 19 18 17 16 15 14 13 12

Acknowledgement

Every book is an authentic collective gift. This one is no different, and I want to thank Jim Peoples and Diane Miller personally for being the kind of wonderful, caring human beings that they are as publishers. They are truly the future. This book could not have been done without their patience, encouragement, and philosophy. Each book is unique, and that uniqueness is made so much better by the expert work of editors. My editor, Charmaine Harris-Stewart, has an eye for seeing the invisible, a necessary talent of a good editor. I am very grateful to her for the time she has spent working on this project.

The Peoples Publishing Group has assembled an outstanding group of professionals. I wish to thank them for their dedication and hard work.

Dr. Molefi Kete Asante

Writers

Theresa Flynn-Nason
Reading Specialist
Voorhees Middle School
Voorhees, NJ

David J. Glunt
Social Studies Teacher
Tree of Life High School
Columbus, OH

Contributors

Barbara Brown Gathers
Social Studies Gifted Program
Lenox Academy
Brooklyn, NY

Augusta Mann
Consultant in Education
IA Systems Inc.
New York, NY

Dr. Judylynn Bailey-Mitchell
Principal
Wicomico County School District
Salisbury, MD

Pamela McKay
Professor of Social Studies
North Division High School
Milwaukee, WI

Gerianne Francis Scott
Professor of English
Language Arts
Roberto Clemente Junior
High School, CIS 166
Bronx, NY

Michael Williams
Teacher: Social Studies/
Language Arts
Community Action School IS 258
New York NY 10025

Creative Team

Editor, Charmaine Harris-Stewart

Instructional Design, Augusta Mann,
Charmaine Harris-Stewart

Pre-Press & Production Manager, Doreen Smith

Project Manager & Page Makeup, Amy Koval

Desktop Publishing Assistant, Roy Caratozzolo

Designer, John Marmolejos

Copy Editors, Shelly Rawson, Scott Caffrey,
Wayne Martelli

Permissions Manager, Kristine Liebman

Cover Design, Michele Sakow

Publisher, Diane Miller

Cover Illustration, Charles Lilly

••

On The Cover
Mt. Freedom
Front (L to R) Harriet Tubman, Frederick Douglass,
Dr. Martin Luther King, Jr.
Back (L to R) W. E. B. Du Bois, Mary McLeod-
Bethune, Marcus Garvey

The Artist Speaks
"Just as our ancient African ancestors once carved magnificent images of the great pharaohs in stone, Mt. Freedom inspired me to represent that same greatness with the Rev. Martin Luther King, Jr., and others equally as great in rock for all ages."
Charles Lilly (Nyatafa Nutala)

About the Artist
Charles Lilly, recently renamed Nyatafa (a man of integrity) Nutala (artist) holds numerous certificates of merit from the prestigious Society of Illustrators, New York; several awards from the Art Director's Club, New York; and awards of merit from the Society of Publication Designers. His work was prominently featured at the 22nd Annual Black Caucus Legislative Weekend in Washington and in African American museums and galleries. Clients include the NAACP and the United Negro College Fund, as well as many Fortune 500 corporations. Nyatafa Nutala is a single parent raising his 18-year old son, Eliott, who he calls his "greatest work of art." Young Eliott is following in his father's footsteps. Throughout high school, he has received numerous art awards, and recently he has received a full four-year scholarship to the School of Visual Arts, New York.

DEDICATION

To those bold school boards and superintendents who have had the courage to ask new questions. They have inspired me and have moved me to write.

Dr. Molefi Kete Asante

....

ENDORSEMENTS

PEDAGOGICALLY SOUND

*"**African American History: A Journey of Liberation** reflects the collective struggle of African people for development and then, because of colonization and enslavement, for liberation and reconstruction.*

The book is organized in a way that is pedagogically sound. Especially important is the sophisticated use of maps for orientation. The narrative is inviting and the scholarly foundation is substantial."

Dr. Asa G. Hillard, III
Department of Educational Policy Studies
Georgia State University
Atlanta, GA

IMPRESSIVE

*"The second edition of **African American History: A Journey of Liberation** is even more impressive than the first. Teachers have at their fingertips critical, accurate, and pertinent information about the active participation of African Americans in our history. The text integrates social studes, cultural themes, pedagogical aids and highly motivating activities that will engage students in the process of learning their own history. Finally, a history book that conveys, in a reader-friendly way, what we've always known: African Americans have a voice and place in American history."*

Debra A. Braithwaite,
Deputy Superintendent, Curriculum and Instruction
New York, NY

REFRESHING

*"**African American History: A Journey of Liberation** by Dr. Molefi Kete Asante is a remarkably refreshing book for students of all cultures. The book is full of illustrative examples, historical portraits, useful facts, and pedagogical aids. It represents an educational achievement of the highest level, and will be used in classrooms throughout the nation for many years to come."*

Dr. Marta Moreno Vega, President
Caribbean Cultural Center/African Diaspora Institute
New York, NY

A REAL TRIUMPH

"What a triumph it is to finally open a textbook and find the African and African American experience portrayed accurately and with dignity as only Molefi Asante can do. Each page turned is a triumph for the African and African American experience. Now students everywhere will read, view pictures, and study timelines that portray African American history in an accurate and dignified way. Thank you Molefi Asante!"

Kay Lovelace Taylor,
Educational Consultant
KLT & Associates
Gibbsboro, NJ

ABOUT THE AUTHOR

Dr. Molefi Kete Asante is a professor in the Department of African American Studies at Temple University—the premier center of graduate training in African American Studies. Considered by his peers to be one of the most distinguished contemporary scholars, Asante is the author or editor of 47 books, including the best-selling *The Egyptian Philosophers* (2000), *The African American Atlas* (1999), *Transcultural Realities* (2001), and the novel *Scattered to the Wind* (2001).

He has published more scholarly books than any contemporary African American scholar and has been recently recognized as one of the ten most widely cited African Americans. In addition, *Black Issues in Higher Education* recognized him as one of the most influential leaders in the past 15 years. Dr. Asante received his Ph.D. from UCLA at the age of 26 and was appointed to the position of full professor at the age of 30 at the State University of New York at Buffalo. He joined Temple University's faculty in 1984 and created the first Ph.D. program in African American Studies. During his career, he has been the director of more than 65 doctoral dissertations at UCLA, SUNY-Buffalo, and Temple. He has written more than 200 articles for educational and social science journals and magazines and is the founder of the theory of Afrocentricity.

Utne Reader magazine listed him as "one of the 100 Leading Thinkers in America," and Asante was recommended in a survey as one of the 25 most influential African American male leaders of the last 200 years. He has been called "the most influential professor in black America." In April 2000, Dr. Asante was prominently featured in the TNT documentary "Faces of Evil," where he explained the brutality of the European Slave Trade and African enslavement. He has also appeared on programs such as: *Nightline, Nighttalk, BET, MacNeil-Lehrer News Hour, Today Show,* the *Tony Brown Show, Night Watch, Like It Is* and *60 Minutes.* He is President of the African Historical Organization and the ANKH Institute, and convener of the annual Cheikh Anta Diop Conference on African and African American Studies.

In 1995, he was made a traditional king, Nana Okru Asante Peasah, Kyldomhene of Tafo, in Ghana. Dr. Asante has been, or is presently, a consultant for the school districts of Detroit, Birmingham, Los Angeles, New York, Trenton, Baltimore, Camden, Cleveland, the Virgin Islands, New Orleans, and Gary, Indiana on cultural and professional development. He has given presentations at ten of the top educational conferences and professional meetings during the past five years. An activist-scholar, he believes it is not enough to know—one must act to humanize the world.

REVIEWERS AND CONSULTANTS

Herb Boyd is an historian, journalist, author, and activist who has written and edited nine books including *The Autobiography of a People—Three Centuries of African American History Told by Those Who Lived It.* He teaches creative nonfiction at New York University, and African and African American history at the College of New Rochelle, School of New Resources, New Rochelle, NY.

Booker T. Coleman, Jr. is a teacher, consultant, staff developer, and curriculum writer of African American history and culture and indigenous American history and culture. Currently, he is a staff developer in social studies and cultural education at the Diana Sands Educational Complex, Bronx, NY.

Dr. Rosalind Robinson Jeffries is a historian and an art history expert who specializes in anthropology and studio art, museum studies, art history, and African and African American art history. Dr. Jeffries was the Director of Education for the Center of African Art, now called the Museum of African Art. She was also the Coordinator of Traveling Exhibitions in the African Art Department and Community Education Department at the Metropolitan Museum of Art in New York City. She teaches art and African American studies at Jersey City State College, Jersey City, NJ. She is also a professor in humanities at the School of Visual Arts, New York, NY.

INTRODUCTION BY THE AUTHOR
Dr. Molefi Kete Asante

I clearly remember the time I first met Malcolm X. It was August 1963. It was after I had met Martin Luther King, Jr. The setting was a small restaurant in Washington, D.C., and the great man walked into the crowded space and waited like everyone else to be served. Looking over at my table, he pointed his finger at me and said, "Don't you forget your history."

Not forgetting my history is the reason that I found this book, *African American History: A Journey of Liberation*, to be the most exciting project I have ever undertaken. It flows from my belief that the records regarding African Americans must be examined from the inside, from the standpoint of African people as active agents of history—not objects on the fringes of Europe. This book is a new history or historiography, a new way of writing about history.

I have not forgotten my history but, instead, have worked on ways to improve the transmission of that history to others. African American history is not static, but dynamic, moving us through time transgenerationally and transcontinentally. Students who read this book are introduced to the origins of the African American population, its many cultural streams, and its rich legacy of resistance to injustice and inequality. They find themselves in the presence of the authentic voices of the African people and, for the first time, see the honest achievements, failures, and victories of a people who were transported across the sea to the Americas and the Caribbean. There is true nobility here. In the United States, that nobility is woven into the tapestry of our nation, stretching from the Atlantic Ocean to the Pacific across a land in which African people have embedded their own designs.

My task in writing this book was to capture the African agency, the action, and the excitement of this marvelous history. Too often, when I conduct workshops for schoolteachers and we talk about the significant events in our nation's history, the first events (in their minds) are ones created by Europeans, rather than by Africans or African Americans. After we discuss the need to view African American history from an African center, and then rethink and retalk our knowledge of history, the joy that invitably swells up from this new African-centered focus is amazing to me. It is the joy of ownership—of seeing oneself and one's ancestors as active agents who create and change the history of this nation—that overflows and stimulates a hunger to know more. It is the same joy your students will know when they see that the ownership of this history belongs to them. It is a strong American voice that has been left out of the other histories that students have experienced; it is a history written from inside an African center and with an African-centered voice; it sings the praises of our ancestors as it tells the honest story of the African American in this country. By understanding the history of our ancestors, we can gain valuable insight about our present and future.

No, I have not forgotten my history. Join me now on a journey of great anguish and great joy. We have persevered on this journey of liberation, and I hope that, in the telling of this story from an African-centered voice, the journey will come alive in all its nobility and majesty and will be a liberating experience for every reader.

Culture is a lens through which we view our lives. It provides us with a sense of reality. It helps us interpret the world. As the author of this textbook, Dr. Molefi Asante, explains, "Culture refers to the learned and shared values, perceptions, attitudes, predispositions, and behavior patterns of a human group which allow people to organize experiences in certain ways."

One of Dr. Asante's primary purposes for writing *African American History: A Journey of Liberation* is to provide students with a history told by an African voice, from an African center. His goal is to enable students to see themselves and African American people as agents in the making of history. When reading content-area textbooks, students need to be able to easily organize the information and see a connection to what they already know. The infusion of African American cultural themes in the exercises in this Worktext provides students with an instructional design that deepens the connection between history and their world, and in so doing, helps them experience more fully Dr. Asante's centering philosophy.

AFRICAN AMERICAN CULTURAL THEMES

African American scholars have identified a list of themes that are important in African and African American culture. Of these there are nine major themes:

- **Spirituality**—a recognition and emphasis on spiritual forces in life; a focus on the belief in a higher power and universal order

- **Resilience**—the ability to bounce back from disappointment, oppression, and disaster to renew life's energy and continue forward

- **Humanism**—a concern for human beings, their condition, interests, and achievements

- **Communalism**—a sense of community; a coming together of a people

- **Orality and Verbal Expressiveness**—knowledge that is passed on through word of mouth and the cultivation of a unique and skillful oratorical style designed to impress and persuade others

- **Realness**—the need to face life the way it is without pretense; understanding life and telling it "like it is"

- **Personal Style and Uniqueness**—the cultivation of a unique or distinctive personality; putting one's own creative stamp on an activity

- **Emotional Vitality**—an expression of liveliness and openness conveyed in the language, oral literature, song, dance, body language, and folk poetry of a people

- **Musicality/Rhythm**—demonstrates the connectedness of movement, music, dance, percussiveness, and rhythm, personified through the musical beat

TABLE OF CONTENTS

WORKTEXT AFRICAN AMERICAN HISTORY: A JOURNEY OF LIBERATION

Second Edition

UNIT 5 AFRICANS AND THE AMERICANS' WARS WITH BRITAIN

UNIT 6 FREE AFRICANS

UNIT 7 CONTESTING ENSLAVEMENT

UNIT 8 STRIKING FOR LIBERTY AGAIN

UNIT 9   THE RECONSTRUCTION YEARS

Writing an Editorial

UNIT 10   TURN OF THE CENTURY

Writing a Script

UNIT 11   STAND UP FOR YOUR RIGHTS

Document-Based Practice

UNIT 12   WE WILL NEVER TURN BACK

Writing a Campaign Speech

UNIT 13   THE FREEDOM MOVEMENT'S MARCH ON LIBERTY

UNIT 14   WINNING THROUGH LAW

UNIT 15   AN ERA OF INDIGNATION

UNIT 16   PROGRESS AND PROVISIONS

Note-taking Tips | **PREWRITING**

Write your notes in outline form in your own words.

Review this unit about ancestors. Decide whom you would like to interview to write an essay about the ancestry of a person you know. Use the note-taking chart below to help you organize the answers to your interview questions.

Date: _____ Name of Person Interviewed: _____

Who:
Find out four details that make the subject of your interview interesting.

Who: _____

_____

_____

_____

What:
Find out four details that back up the main ideas of the first paragraph.

What: _____

_____

_____

_____

Where:
Find out where this ancestor lived with some details about the location and the people who live there.

Where: _____

_____

_____

_____

When:
Find out the time periods that cover the life events of this ancestor.

When: _____

_____

_____

_____

Why:
Explain why you selected this person. What makes his or her life story special and important to share with others?

Why: _____

_____

_____

_____

_____

_____

DRAFTING

Drafting Tips

Use your notes to prepare your first draft.

Use your note-taking chart on page 1 to help you draft your one-page essay on the ancestry of a person you know. Remember to include enough interesting and informative details to make the audience feel as if they have actually met the individual.

Introduction:
Begin your essay with a general introduction of the person you interviewed.

Introduction: _____

_____

_____

_____

_____

Main Ideas:
The first sentence of each paragraph, the topic sentence, should clearly state a main idea or detail about the person you interviewed.

Main Ideas: _____

_____

_____

_____

_____

Supporting Ideas:
The remaining sentences in each paragraph should support the main idea. The final sentence or two of each paragraph should tie your thoughts together.

Supporting Ideas: _____

_____

_____

_____

_____

Quotations:
You may want to quote the person you interviewed to add life and realism to your essay.

Quotations: _____

_____

_____

_____

_____

Conclusion:
End your essay with a concluding paragraph that restates or sums up your main ideas.

Conclusion: _____

_____

_____

_____

_____

Revising and Proofreading Tips

Polish and clean up your writing as you prepare for publication.

Organization:

Make sure you have written a well-organized essay that includes an introduction, several supporting paragraphs, and a conclusion.

Edit:

Anything in your essay that does not add to your topic and main ideas should be removed.

Sentence Length:

Use some shorter, simple sentences between complex and compound ones.

Word Choice:

Have you used the best words to convey your meaning? Focus on choosing the best possible verbs and adjectives.

Check Your Style:

Fix any sentences that are choppy or awkward.

Proofread:

Check for problems with grammar, usage, punctuation, capitalization, and spelling.

REVISING AND PROOFREADING

When you revise your essay, make sure that you have included all the main points and supporting details that describe the ancestry of the person you interviewed. Review your note-taking chart to make sure that you have not omitted any important information. Revise your essay on the lines below.

_____

_____

_____

_____

_____

_____

_____

_____

_____

_____

_____

_____

_____

_____

_____

_____

_____

_____

_____

_____

_____

_____

_____

_____

_____

_____

_____

_____

_____

Publishing Tips	**PUBLISHING**

Prepare your essay for publication.

Copy the clean, final version of your essay on the lines below. With your teacher's help, decide how you want to "publish" your essay. You may want to post it on the classroom bulletin board, make a class scrapbook entitled "Ancestry," or read your essay to the class.

Visual Appeal:

Check your finished product to make sure it is visually appealing. The margins should be uniform and the lines evenly spaced. If you want to post your essay, it should be written in clear, bold letters. Use a dark ink pen, rather than pencil or red pen. Make sure the title is in large print so that it stands out.

Adding Graphics:

Consider adding a graphic to enhance the "look" of your final product. Possible graphics include a photograph of the person you interviewed, a family tree that traces the person's ancestors, or a world map that illustrates the counties those ancestors emigrated from.

Visual Literacy

Review the photograph and key ideas presented in the Unit 1 Summary. This photograph is repeated on page 5 of your textbook. Which key idea does it reinforce? Write a caption that links the photograph to the unit title and the key idea in this unit.

Caption: _____

_____

_____

_____

Historical Context

Using information from the text and photos and captions in the Origins color visuals on pages A1–A8, write an essay based on the bulleted items.

Compose your essay on separate paper.

- Provide examples of Africa's contributions to the world.

- Discuss the African concept of spirituality.

- Compare the positive perception of Africans in the "African Presence in Europe" section with the negative stereotypes of Africans and African Americans in America.

Student Traveler

In small groups, research modern-day Timbuktu. Then use your findings to respond to the following questions.

Chapter 4 ends with a discussion of the renowned 16th century scholar, Ahmed Baba, vice chancellor of the University of Sankore, in the city of Timbuktu. A center of commerce, religion, and scholarship, Timbuktu was one of the most advanced cities in the world during the late 1500s. Prepare to visit present-day Timbuktu. Although this once impressive city is now a gray mud-brick town in the country of Mali, its streets resonate with powerful memories of the past.

1. What did your group find most interesting about the history of Timbuktu and its historical sites? _____

_____

2. List the brochures and reading materials that you collected.

_____

_____

3. With whom did you talk or meet to get information? _____

_____

_____

4. In what ways did they help you? _____

_____

African American Cultural Themes

Conduct research to learn about the spiritual meanings and functions of the Step Pyramid, the Great Sphinx, and the Great Pyramid at Giza. Create a booklet with drawings and summaries of information about each of these three monuments. Use the space provided to plan your booklet.

You may use the blank pages at the back of the Worktext if you need additional space.

Human history began in Africa, and the first human migrations were made by the African people as they traveled in groups to the northern and eastern parts of the continent. Unit 1 highlights four of the nine African American cultural themes that were a part of the African social experience beginning in ancient times.

- **Personal Style and Uniqueness**—the cultivation of a unique or distinctive personality; putting one's own creative stamp on an activity
- **Humanism**—a concern for human beings, their condition, interests, and achievements
- **Communalism**—a sense of community; a coming together of a people
- **Spirituality**—a recognition and emphasis on spiritual forces in life; a focus on the belief in a higher power and universal order

In Unit 1, the author writes about the strength and spirit of the African people. He introduces the civilizations of the Nile Valley and the great West African empires and describes their grand achievements in architecture (personal style and uniqueness), government, agriculture, land and sea exploration, social organizations (humanism and communalism), education, and religion. Religious achievement is clearly evident in the deeply spiritual people of Kemet, who built three architectural wonders—pictured on page A4 of your textbook—that stand as monuments to the spiritual forces in their lives (spirituality).

BOOKLET

Drawings	Summary

Note-taking Tips | PREWRITING

Note cards are a good way to organize your writing.

Record Your Sources:

Keep a bibliography that includes the title of your sources, the name of each author, the date of publication, and the page numbers where you gathered information.

Subtopics:

Each note card should contain a subtopic that is very specific. This will help you arrange your topics as you begin to write.

Paraphrase:

While taking notes, you do not need to write in complete sentences, but the information you write down should be complete enough to make sense of later.

Review this unit about the European Slave Trade and research a specific African port city to write a one-page report. Refer to the Center your Writing exercise on page 65 of your textbook for more details. Create additional note cards like the one below to help you organize your information.

Port City:_____

Title:_____ Author:_____

Publisher:_____

Copyright Date:_____ Pages: _____

Subtopic: _____

_____

Notes: _____

_____

_____

_____

_____

_____

_____

_____

_____

_____

_____

_____

_____

_____

_____

_____

Drafting Tips

DRAFTING

Use your notes to prepare the first draft.

Use your note cards to help you draft the report on the European Slave Trade. Organize the cards in the order that you want to present the information.

Introduction:

Begin with an opening paragraph that identifies the topic of your report.

Introduction: _____

_____

_____

_____

_____

Main Idea:

Use this question to state the main idea of your report.

What was special about this port city and the people who live there?

_____

_____

_____

Supporting Details:

Use this question to develop your first supporting detail.

Where and how were the Africans captured?

_____

_____

_____

_____

Supporting Details:

Use this question to develop your second supporting detail.

How many slave ships set sail per year, and what was their destination?

_____

_____

_____

_____

Conclusion:

Use this question to develop a concluding paragraph that restates or sums up your main idea.

Why was this port city important to the slave trade?

_____

_____

_____

_____

Revising and Proofreading Tips

REVISING AND PROOFREADING

This step is important in producing a clear and interesting report. Review your note cards to make sure that you have not omitted any important information. Revise your report on the lines below.

Polish and clean up your writing as you prepare for publication.

Organization:

Check to make sure you have written a well-organized report that includes an introduction, several supporting paragraphs, and a conclusion.

Edit:

Anything in your report that does not add to your topic and main ideas (subtopics) should be removed.

Sentence Length:

Use some shorter, simple sentences between complex and compound ones.

Word Choice:

Have you used the best words to convey your meaning? Focus on choosing the best possible verbs and adjectives.

Check Your Style:

Fix any sentences that are choppy or awkward.

Proofread:

Check for problems with grammar, usage, punctuation, capitalization, and spelling.

Publishing Tips	PUBLISHING

Prepare your report for publication.

Copy a clean, final version of your report on the lines below. With your teacher's help, decide how you want to "publish" your report. You may want to post it on the classroom bulletin board, add it to your journal or writing portfolio, or read it to the class.

Visual Appeal:

Check your finished product to make sure it is visually appealing. The margins should be uniform and the lines evenly spaced. If you want to post your report, it should be written in clear, bold letters. Use a dark ink pen, rather than pencil or red pen. Make sure the title is in large print so that it stands out.

Adding Graphics:

Consider adding a graphic—such as a photograph, an illustration, or a map—to enhance the "look" of your final product.

Create a Book:

You and a few of your classmates may want to compile several reports into a booklet to better understand the experience of producing a collaborative work.

Visual Literacy

Review the images and key ideas in the Unit 2 Summary. Which key ideas do the images reinforce? Write a caption that links these images to the unit title and the key ideas in the unit.

Caption:_____

_____

_____

Historical Context

Using information from Unit 2 and the events listed on the unit and chapter timelines, write an essay based on the bulleted items.

Compose your essay on separate paper.

- Summarize the events that occurred between the time the Portuguese slave trade begins and the period when Portugal, Spain, England, and Holland lead the Slave Trade.

- Discuss the major theme that emerges from this period.

- Conclude your essay with a discussion of the economic, moral, and ethical issues surrounding this period.

Student Traveler

Imagine that you are an African who wants to keep alive your memories of this experience by creating an oral history. Research the African port cities and records of the slave trade to develop the details of your capture, enslavement, and journey to America. Use the following questions to guide your research. Then study your answers and relate your oral history to the class.

Chapter 6 relates the "Dreaded Middle Passage" that brought many enslaved Africans to the Americas. The high death rate on these voyages suggests that the Africans who survived must have been very strong at the outset. Many details of these passages have been lost, but from the records that remain, you can construct a meaningful account.

1. What was your life like in Africa? _____

_____

_____

2. How were you captured and brought to the slave trader?

_____

_____

3. What were the hardships of the Middle Passage? How did you survive? _____

_____

4. Where were you sold in America? to whom?_____

_____

African American Cultural Themes

Working in small groups, plan a mutiny aboard a slave ship. Discuss how and when you will execute the mutiny. Discuss the choices you must make if the mutiny fails. Have each person write a brief letter about what any of the survivors should tell your family, if the mutiny succeeds but you die. Explain how the African American cultural themes of resilience, humanism, and spirituality directed your actions. Use the space provided to plan your mutiny and write your letter.

In this Unit, the author describes the circumstances that led to the European Slave Trade, the beginning of dehumanization of Africans by Europeans, and the horrors of the Middle Passage.

- **Resilience**—the ability to bounce back from disappointment, oppression, and disaster to renew life's energy and continue forward
- **Spirituality**—a recognition and emphasis on spiritual forces in life; a focus on the belief in a higher power and universal order
- **Humanism**—a concern for human beings, their condition, interests, and achievements

The Africans' record of survival, resistance, and mutinies aboard the slave ships demonstrated their refusal to be defeated (resilience). Others responded by jumping overboard and releasing their lives to a higher power (spirituality) rather than submit to the hardship and inhumane conditions of enslavement (humanism).

Who: _____

_____

What: _____

_____

Where: _____

_____

When: _____

_____

How: _____

_____

Choices: _____

_____

_____

_____

_____

_____

Date: _____

Dear _____

_____

_____

_____

_____

_____

_____

_____

_____

_____

_____

Part A
Answering Document-Based Questions

Note-taking Tips

Document-Based Questions test your ability to analyze a group of documents.

Word Choice:

Focus on how the choice of words expresses the writer's attitude toward the subject.

Theme:

Review the definition of "resilience," one of the nine African American cultural themes.

Analyze:

A painting is a powerful communication tool. Pay close attention to details such as body language, setting and scenery, and background items. Reflect on the message these details send to an observer.

Consider:

Sometimes a popular saying arises out of a people's common experience. Such a saying, through the wisdom it holds, can unite a people and give them a means to persevere through hard times.

Review this unit about how enslaved Africans endured a horrific existence in Colonial America. Many Africans drew upon survival skills to help cope with the brutality of enslavement.

Directions: The following questions are based on primary sources in Unit 3 that illustrate Africans' survival skills. Review each source and answer the questions that follow.

Document #1: Analyzing a Poem (Page 79)
Review the excerpt from the Paul Laurence Dunbar poem.

1. How does the speaker cope with enslavement?

_____

_____

2. How does the speaker's action demonstrate resilience?

_____

_____

Document #2: Analyzing a Painting and Caption (Page 71)
Review the Jacob Lawrence painting *Old Plantation*, and read the caption. Answer the following questions based on your observations.

1. How do the Africans shown in the painting cope with enslavement?

_____

_____

2. How do these actions demonstrate resilience?

_____

_____

Document #3: Analyzing an Adage (Page 90)
"Learn to work work or work will work you."

1. According to this adage, what is the best way to cope with the harsh labor practices of enslavement?

_____

_____

Part B
Drafting A Document-Based Essay

Drafting Tips

Begin with a prewriting strategy such as a concept map or Venn diagram.

Historical Context: Enslaved Africans showed their resilience by employing survival skills to cope with their captivity.

Task: Reflect on the messages communicated in the documents from page 13. Write a well-organized essay in which you discuss the following:

- why members of modern society need survival skills even though enslavement no longer exists

- an incident in which you demonstrated resilience by using one of the survival skills noted in the documents

Analysis:

Think about the similarities and differences between the documents.

Analysis: _____

_____

_____

_____

Thesis Statement:

Write a thesis statement that identifies the topic of your essay. Be careful not to simply restate the topic.

Thesis Statement: _____

_____

_____

_____

Supporting Ideas:

Generate a list of details that support your thesis statement.

Supporting Ideas: _____

_____

_____

_____

_____

_____

_____

_____

Conclusion:

End your essay with a concluding paragraph that restates or sums up your main ideas.

Conclusion: _____

_____

_____

_____

_____

Revising and Proofreading Tips

REVISING AND PROOFREADING

Polish and clean up your writing as you prepare for publication.

When you revise your essay, make sure that you have addressed each topic. Go back and read each bulleted statement to be sure. Make sure you have used all the important information from your notes. Revise your essay on the lines below.

Organization:

Check to make sure you have written a well-organized essay that includes an introduction, several supporting paragraphs, and a conclusion.

Edit:

Anything in your essay that does not add to your topic and main ideas should be removed.

Sentence Length:

Make sure you have varied the length of your sentences between short, medium, and long.

Word Choice:

Have you used the best words to convey your meaning? Focus on choosing the best possible verbs and adjectives.

Check Your Style:

Fix any sentences that are choppy or awkward.

Proofread:

Check for problems with grammar, usage, punctuation, capitalization, and spelling.

_____
_____
_____
_____
_____
_____
_____
_____
_____
_____
_____
_____
_____
_____
_____
_____
_____
_____
_____
_____
_____
_____
_____
_____

Publishing Tips

PUBLISHING

Prepare your essay for publication.

Copy the clean, final version of your essay on the lines below and add a title. With your teacher's help, decide how you want to "publish" your essay. You may want to post it on the classroom bulletin board, make a class scrapbook or writing portfolio, or read it to the class.

Visual Appeal:

Check your finished product to make sure it is visually appealing. The margins should be uniform and the lines evenly spaced. If you want to post your essay, it should be written in clear, bold letters. Use a dark ink pen, rather than pencil or red pen. Make sure the title is in large print so that it stands out.

Adding Graphics:

Consider adding a graphic—such as a photograph, an illustration, or a map— to enhance the "look" of your final product.

Visual Literacy

Review the key ideas presented in the Unit 3 Summary. Then carefully observe sculptor Edmonia Lewis's work *Forever Free* on page B8 of the Journey color visuals. Which key idea does the sculpture reinforce? Write a caption that links this work to the unit title and the key idea in this unit.

Caption: _____

_____

_____

_____

_____

Historical Context

Using information from the text and *The Banjo Lesson* on page B6 of the Journey color visuals, write an essay that addresses each bulleted item.

Compose your essay on separate paper.

- Identify how the painting depicts African cultural traditions.
- Explain how cultural traditions foster centeredness.
- Make a connection between centeredness and survival skills.

Student Traveler

Work with classmates to create a travelogue that provides travelers with the historical significance and locations of these sites. Begin by writing a one-sentence description of each site. Attach all reference materials collected to the completed travelogue.

Write your travelogue on separate paper.

In Chapter 12, you read about one of the most well-known African freedom fighters—Harriet Tubman. The Harriet Tubman Coalition in Cambridge, Maryland, offers a tour of four sites that document Harriet Tubman's life and work. The tour includes the items listed below.

Long Wharf: _____

_____

_____

Bazzel Methodist Episcopal Church: _____

_____

_____

The Stanley Institute: _____

_____

_____

Brodas Plantation: _____

_____

African American Cultural Themes

Working in a small group, discuss the meaning of this quote found on page 77 in Chapter 8 of your textbook.

"African culture was resilient because the people themselves were resilient. Time after time they bounced back from the harshest of circumstances."

Keeping in mind the meaning of this quote, create a script for a one-act play about two resilient, enslaved Africans who, despite great hardships, refused to give up and finally escaped to freedom. Use the space provided to plan your play.

Write your play on separate paper.

The traditions and cultures of enslaved Africans were unwelcome in Colonial America. Unit 3 highlights three of the nine African American cultural themes that contributed to their survival through this period.

- **Orality and Verbal Expressiveness**—knowledge that is passed on through word of mouth and the cultivation of a unique and skillful oratorical style designed to impress and persuade others
- **Communalism**—a sense of community; a coming together of a people
- **Resilience**—the ability to bounce back from disappointment, oppression, and disaster to renew life's energy and continue forward

In Unit 3, the author shows how, in spite of extremely difficult circumstances, Africans held onto their cultural traditions. Through storytelling and other oral traditions (orality and verbal expressiveness), the elders transmitted positive values and maintained a spirit of community (communalism) from one generation to another. Continuing a legacy of perseverance and resistance to enslavement, enslaved Africans consistently planned and carried out revolts and escapes (resilience and communalism).

ACT I

Title: _____

_____

_____

Setting: _____

_____

_____

Scene: _____

_____

_____

_____

_____

_____

Character 1: _____

_____

_____

Character 2: _____

_____

_____

Character 1: _____

_____

_____

Character 2: _____

_____

_____

Note-taking Tips | PREWRITING

Use the following tips for each source.

Refer to the Center Your Writing activity on page 141 of your textbook. In Unit 4, you discovered that Nat Turner led the most serious African uprising in U.S. history. The rebellion triggered certain reactions among southern white leaders of the time. Use a variety of reference tools to gather additional information about Nat Turner and the rebellion he led. Focus on the reactions it triggered and how modern historians and African Americans view this leader and his legacy. Use the note-taking chart below to help you organize your research findings.

Record Your Sources:

Start a bibliography that includes the title of your sources, the name of each author, the date of publication, and the page numbers where you gathered information.

Paraphrase:

Write the main idea obtained from each source in your own words.

When Using Quotes:

When you use a quotation, you need to include the name of the person being quoted.

Source 1: _____

_____

_____

_____

Source 2: _____

_____

_____

_____

Source 3: _____

_____

_____

_____

Source 4: _____

_____

_____

_____

Drafting Tips

DRAFTING

Use your notes to prepare the first draft.

Use your note-taking chart on page 19 to help you draft a four-paragraph report on Nat Turner. Remember to begin each paragraph with the lead sentence provided. Each lead sentence serves as the topic sentence or main idea of the paragraph. Use the research findings noted in your chart to generate the supporting details.

Main Idea:

The first sentence of each paragraph, the topic sentence, is provided for you. This report consists of three main ideas.

Main Idea: Nat Turner's rebellion shocked southern white leaders and led to the following actions.

Supporting Details: _____

_____

_____

_____

_____

Main Idea: Some historians say that Turner's religious zeal was fanaticism.

Supporting Details:

The remaining sentences in each paragraph should support the main idea. The final sentence or two of each paragraph should tie your thoughts together.

Supporting Details: _____

_____

_____

_____

Main Idea: To African Americans, Nat Turner was a hero.

Supporting Details: _____

_____

_____

_____

_____

Conclusion:

End your report with a concluding paragraph that restates or sums up your main ideas.

Conclusion: _____

_____

_____

_____

_____

Revising and Proofreading Tips

Polish and clean up your writing as you prepare for publication.

Organization:

Make sure each paragraph has enough details to support the main idea and that you have written a strong conclusion.

Edit:

Anything in your report that does not add to your topic and main ideas should be removed.

Sentence Length:

Use some shorter, simple sentences between complex and compound ones.

Word Choice:

Have you used the best words to convey your meaning? Focus on choosing the best possible verbs and adjectives.

Check Your Style:

Fix any sentences that are choppy or awkward.

Proofread:

Check for problems with grammar, usage, punctuation, capitalization, and spelling.

REVISING AND PROOFREADING

When you revise your report, make sure that you have included all the lead sentences and supporting details that describe the rebellion. Review your note-taking chart to make sure that you have not omitted any important information. Revise your report on the lines below.

_____

_____

_____

_____

_____

_____

_____

_____

_____

_____

_____

_____

_____

_____

_____

_____

_____

_____

_____

_____

_____

_____

_____

_____

Publishing Tips	**PUBLISHING**

Prepare your report for publication.

Copy the clean, final version of your report on the lines below. With your teacher's help decide how you want to "publish" your report. You may want to read it to your class, create a writing portfolio, make a class scrapbook entitled "The Legacy of Nat Turner," or post it on the bulletin board for others to read.

Visual Appeal:

Check your finished product to make sure it is visually appealing. The margins should be uniform and the lines evenly spaced. If you want to post your essay, it should be written in clear, bold letters. Use a dark ink pen, rather than pencil or red pen. Make sure the title is in large print so that it stands out.

Adding Graphics:

Consider adding a graphic—such as a photograph, an illustration, or a map—to enhance the "look" of your final product.

_____

_____

_____

_____

_____

_____

_____

_____

_____

_____

_____

_____

_____

_____

_____

_____

_____

_____

_____

_____

_____

_____

Visual Literacy

Review the key ideas presented in the Unit 4 Summary. Then carefully observe the illustration of Nat Turner's capture on page 138. Which key idea does the illustration reinforce? On the lines provided, write a caption that links this illustration to the unit title and the key idea in this unit.

Caption: _____

_____

_____

_____

Historical Context

Using information from the text and the painting, *On to Liberty*, on page B7 of the Journey color visuals, write an essay based on the bulleted items.

Compose your essay on separate paper.

- Identify the form of resistance the painting depicts.

- Explain why some enslaved Africans chose passive resistance as a means of survival.

Student Traveler

Use the Internet and other reference materials to identify the location and historical significance of each site. Record your findings in the space provided.

In Unit 4, you read about the resistance of Africans to American enslavement. Work cooperatively with classmates to learn more about the following historical sites that commemorate African resistance to enslavement.

Stono River Slave Rebellion Historical Marker: _____

_____

_____

Denmark Vesey House: _____

_____

_____

Harpers Ferry National Historic Park: _____

_____

_____

The Amistad Memorial: _____

_____

_____

African American Cultural Themes

There are many biographical books and articles about Harriet Tubman. Working together with other students, read about how her spirituality guided her decisions. Then go back to Chapter 15, pages 138 and 139 of your textbook, and read the description of the spiritual life of Nat Turner. Write an essay comparing and contrasting Turner's spiritual beliefs and experiences with those of Harriet Tubman. Use the space below to plan your essay.

Africans were not willing participants in their enslavement, demonstrating a determination to resist. Unit 4 highlights five of the nine African American cultural themes evident in their resistance.

- **Resilience**
- **Communalism**
- **Spirituality**
- **Orality and Verbal Expressiveness**
- **Humanism**

Refer to page viii for a description of these themes.

In Unit 4, African resistance to the slave trade in Africa, on slave ships, and in the Americas demonstrates the collective strength of the people and their unrelenting struggle for freedom (resilience and communalism). Accounts of the lives and resistance of Denmark Vesey and Nat Turner represent their strong belief in spiritual forces for guidance and support (spirituality), their skillful use of words to persuade others to join their revolt (orality and verbal expressiveness), and their commitment to freedom (humanism).

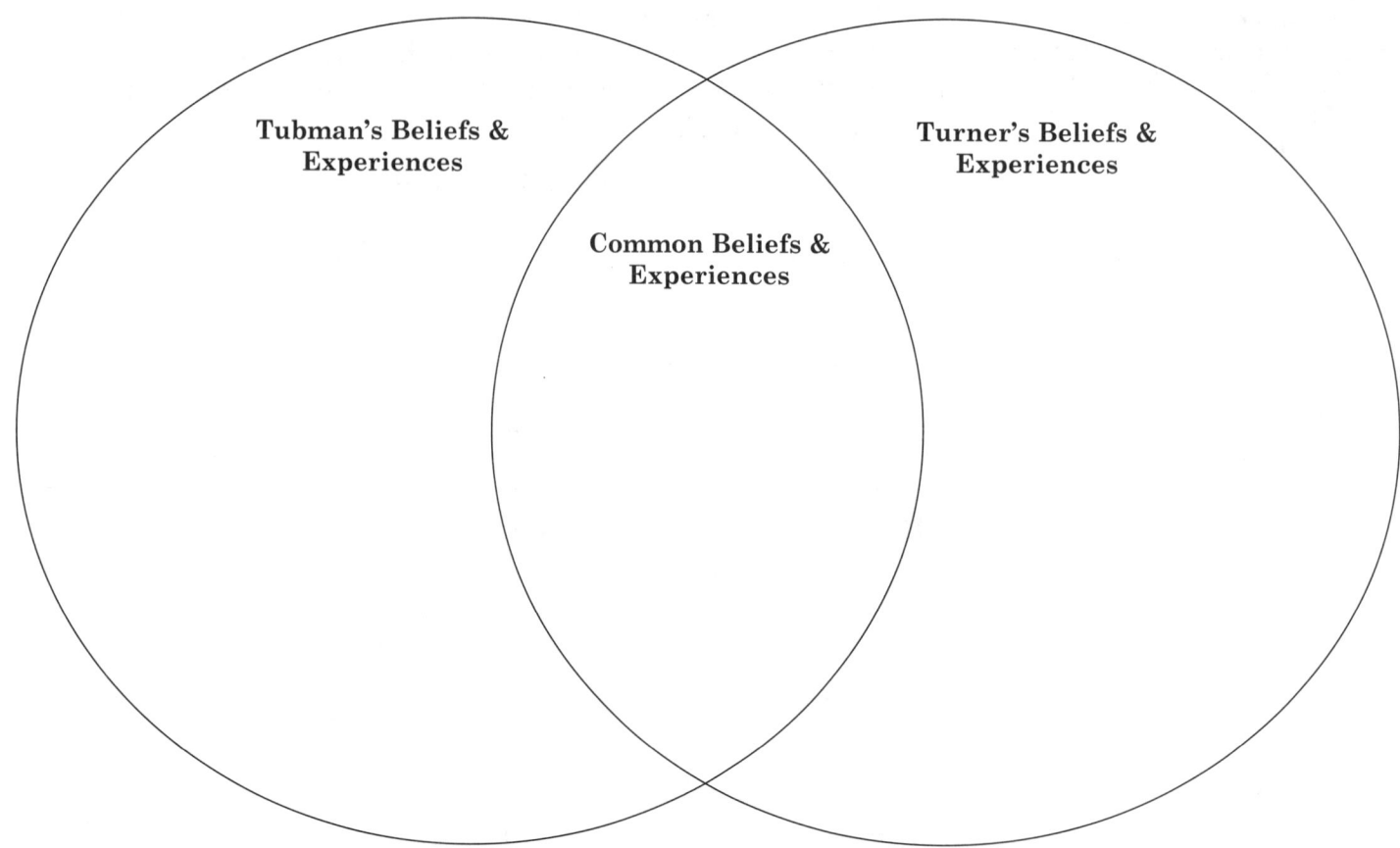

Tubman's Beliefs & Experiences

Turner's Beliefs & Experiences

Common Beliefs & Experiences

Note-taking Tips | PREWRITING

Note-taking Tips

As you gather information, think about the six question words news writers use to develop a story— who, what, when, where, why, and how.

Record Your Sources:

Start a bibliography that includes the title of your sources, the name of each author, the date of publication, and the page numbers where you gathered information.

Paraphrase:

While taking notes, you do not need to write in complete sentences, but the information you write down should be complete enough to make sense later.

References:

If you state a fact directly from a reference source, you need to give credit to the author and the publication.

Refer to the Center Your Writing activity on page 159 of your textbook. In Unit 5, you discovered that Crispus Attucks was the first person to die in a violent incident leading to the Revolutionary War. Three years later, another violent incident, the Boston Tea Party, occurred in Boston Harbor. Use a variety of reference tools to gather additional information about this incident in Boston. Then write a front-page story for *The New York Times*, dated December 17, 1773, describing the incident. Be sure to draw upon your research to provide an historically accurate account of the event. Use the note-taking chart below to help you organize your research findings.

Source 1: _____

_____

_____

_____

_____

Source 2: _____

_____

_____

_____

Source 3: _____

_____

_____

_____

Source 4: _____

_____

_____

_____

_____

| **Drafting Tips** | **DRAFTING** |

Begin with your lead, followed by your facts and details presented in order from the most to the least important.

Use your note-taking chart on page 25 to help you draft your news story. Remember to include important events and details to engage your audience.

Headline:

Write a headline that will grab a reader's attention.

Headline: _____

_____

_____

A Compelling Lead:

The lead of a news story is similar to a topic sentence or a thesis statement. It grabs the reader's attention by stating the main idea.

Lead: _____

_____

_____

_____

_____

Organization of Details:

Go through your research notes and organize the information into a story form. Highlight the facts and details you will use in your story, and decide at what point you will use them.

Details: _____

_____

_____

_____

_____

_____

_____

Quotes:

Most news stories use quotes, either direct (word for word) or indirect. Be sure to identify any source(s) that you quote.

Quotes: _____

_____

_____

_____

_____

Conclusion:

End your story with a concluding paragraph that restates or sums up the main ideas.

Conclusion: _____

_____

_____

_____

_____

Revising and Proofreading Tips

REVISING AND PROOFREADING

Polish and clean up your writing as you prepare for publication.

When you revise your news story, make sure that you have included all the main points, facts, and supporting details a reader would want to know. Review your note-taking chart to make sure that you have not omitted any important information. Revise your news story on the lines below.

Organization and Style:

Does your news story flow smoothly as you move from one idea to the next? Read it out loud to make sure it "reads" well. Fix any sentences that are choppy or awkward. Make sure your sentences clearly communicate the facts of your story to the reader.

Edit:

Remove anything that does not add to your topic and main ideas.

Sentence Length:

Generally, news stories are made up of short sentences. To hold the reader's attention, sentences should be clear and direct.

Word Choice:

Choose the best verbs and adjectives to convey your meaning.

Proofread:

Check for problems with grammar, usage, punctuation, capitalization, and spelling.

_____

_____

_____

_____

_____

_____

_____

_____

_____

_____

_____

_____

_____

_____

_____

_____

_____

_____

_____

_____

_____

_____

_____

_____

_____

_____

_____

Publishing Tips

Prepare your news story for publication.

Visual Appeal:

Check your finished product to make sure it is visually appealing. The margins should be uniform and the lines evenly spaced. If you want to post your news story, it should be written in clear, bold letters. Use a dark ink pen, rather than pencil or red pen. Make sure the title is in large print so that it stands out.

Adding Graphics:

Consider adding a graphic—such as a photograph, an illustration, or a map—to enhance the "look" of your final product.

PUBLISHING

Copy the clean, final version of your news story on the lines below. With your teacher's help, decide how you want to "publish" your story. You may want to read it to your class, create a writing portfolio, make a class scrapbook entitled "On This Day," or post it on the bulletin board for others to read.

_____

_____

_____

_____

_____

_____

_____

_____

_____

_____

_____

_____

_____

_____

_____

_____

_____

_____

_____

_____

_____

_____

_____

_____

_____

_____

Visual Literacy

Review the key ideas presented in the Unit 5 Summary. Then carefully observe Alonzo Chappel's painting on page 153. Which key idea does it reinforce? Write a caption on the lines provided that links this work to the unit title and the key idea in this unit.

Caption: _____

_____

_____

_____

Historical Context

Using information from the text, as well as the painting of Absalom Jones and related caption on page B4 of the Journey color visuals, write an essay based on the bulleted items.

Compose your essay on separate paper.

- Describe the life of Absalom Jones.

- Identify his contributions to the African community.

- Explain how the actions of Absalom Jones demonstrate self-determination.

Student Traveler

Gather informational materials about each of the sites listed. Use the information and other reference materials to create a map of the locations you will visit on your walking tour. Be sure to include a key. Begin by filling in the location for each of the sites provided.

Boston, Massachusetts, is a city rich in historical sites related to African Americans. Work cooperatively with classmates to plan a trip to Boston to walk the Black Heritage Trail and visit the monuments, museums, and memorials located there.

The Africa Meeting House: _____

_____

_____

Crispus Attucks Monument, Plaque, and Burial Site:_____

_____

_____

Prince Hall Monument:_____

_____

_____

Abiel Smith School and Museum of Afro-American History:_____

_____

_____

African American Cultural Themes

In Chapter 17, page 161, you read a speech by commander Andrew Jackson. He was speaking to African soldiers after the Battle of New Orleans had been won. Together with a partner, imagine that you are African soldiers who still have no rights in America. You have fought in this battle and are listening to this speech. What are your thoughts? Write your thoughts in a one-page essay entitled "On Hearing Jackson's Speech, A Personal Reflection." Use the space provided to plan your essay.

Groups of Africans argued for the rights of both enslaved and free Africans by submitting petitions to the government. Unit 5 highlights two of the nine African American cultural themes that helped Africans to endure this difficult period.

- **Resilience**—the ability to bounce back from disappointment, oppression, and disaster to renew life's energy and continue forward
- **Humanism**—a concern with human beings, their condition, interests, and achievements

In Unit 5, the author describes how Africans served heroically in America's wars with Britain. The willingness of African soldiers to fight for a country that denied them human rights, and the courage and skill they showed in combat, testify to their hope for a better life and their belief in the ultimate goodness of all humankind (resilience and humanism).

On Hearing Jackson's Speech, A Personal Reflection

Introduction: _____

_____

_____

_____

Supporting Ideas: _____

_____

_____

_____

Supporting Ideas: _____

_____

_____

_____

Conclusion: _____

_____

_____

_____

Note-taking Tips | PREWRITING

Write your notes in outline form in your own words.

Imagine you have just discovered that the federal government is planning to revoke your right to vote (like Pennsylvania did in 1838). Write a speech, based on facts from different sources, that persuades members of Congress to vote against the pending action. Use the form below to help you organize your findings.

Paraphrase:

While taking notes, you do not need to write in complete sentences, but the information you write down should be complete enough to make sense of later.

Fact 1:_____

_____

_____

_____

_____

Choose Your Facts:

During your research, gather at least five facts. Then choose the three facts you believe to be the strongest and most persuasive.

Fact 2:_____

_____

_____

_____

_____

Make Your Case:

Each fact is a supporting detail of your argument and should clearly and convincingly plead your case.

Fact 3:_____

_____

_____

_____

_____

Analyze:

Think about how the words you choose define your tone, which can be serious, humorous, sarcastic, solemn, etc. Reflect on the message a listener will receive based on the words you select.

Fact 4:_____

_____

_____

_____

Fact 5:_____

_____

_____

_____

Drafting Tips | DRAFTING

Choose the best three facts from your notes, the ones that most convincingly plead your case.

Use your notes on page 31 to help you draft your speech. Remember to include all three facts to successfully win over your audience.

Introductory Paragraph:

Begin your speech by enthusiastically greeting your audience. The remainder of this paragraph should clearly state your position on the issue.

Introductory Paragraph: _____
_____
_____
_____
_____

Supporting Paragraphs:

Each of your next three paragraphs should begin with one of your facts. This will give you three topic sentences. The remaining sentences of these paragraphs should provide additional details that show why the fact is important.

Supporting Paragraph: _____
_____
_____
_____

Supporting Paragraph: _____
_____
_____
_____

Supporting Paragraph: _____
_____
_____
_____

Conclusion:

Make sure your speech ends with a concise, but strong, restatement of your position. This is your last chance to persuade your audience that your position is correct—and one that they should adopt for themselves.

Conclusion: _____
_____
_____
_____

Revising and Proofreading Tips

Polish and clean up your speech as you prepare for delivery.

Organization:

Check to make sure you have written a well-organized speech that includes an introduction, several supporting paragraphs, and a conclusion.

Edit:

Anything in your speech that does not add to your topic and main ideas should be removed.

Sentence Length:

Use some shorter, simple sentences between complex and compound ones.

Word Choice:

Have you used the best words to convey your meaning? Focus on choosing the best possible verbs and adjectives.

Check Your Style:

Fix any sentences that are choppy or awkward.

Proofread:

Check for problems with grammar, usage, punctuation, capitalization, and spelling.

REVISING AND PROOFREADING

When you revise your speech, make sure that you have included all the facts your audience needs to know in order to convince them that your position is correct. Review your notes on page 31 to make sure that you have not omitted any important information. Revise your speech on the lines below.

_____

_____

_____

_____

_____

_____

_____

_____

_____

_____

_____

_____

_____

_____

_____

_____

_____

_____

_____

_____

_____

_____

_____

_____

_____

Delivering the Speech

Prepare to deliver your speech to an audience.

Your Delivery:

Practice delivering your speech at home in front of friends or members of your family.

Style:

Use dramatic pauses to highlight powerful sentences in your speech. This technique gives "weight" to your words.

Tone:

To keep your audience interested, vary the pitch and tone of your voice.

Audience:

Keep your eyes focused on the audience as much as you can. If you practiced delivering your speech, you may have memorized parts of it. This will help you to get your eyes off the page.

Your Voice:

Speak loudly and clearly enough so that everyone in the audience can hear you.

Pace Yourself:

Do not speak too fast or too slow.

PUBLISHING

Copy the clean, final version of your speech on the lines below. With your teacher's help, decide how you want to "publish" your speech. In addition to delivering it to the class, you may want to add it to a class scrapbook or writing portfolio, or post it on a class bulletin board for others to read.

_____

_____

_____

_____

_____

_____

_____

_____

_____

_____

_____

_____

_____

_____

_____

_____

_____

_____

_____

_____

_____

Visual Literacy

Review the New Horizons color visual on page C6, the *Benjamin Bannaker Installation*, and the key ideas presented in the Unit 6 Summary. Which key idea does the work of art reinforce? Write a caption on the lines provided that links this image to the unit title and the key idea in this unit.

Caption: _____

_____

_____

_____

_____

Historical Context

Return to pages 176–177 of your textbook. Select one of the African Americans highlighted on these pages and write an essay based on the bulleted items.

Compose your essay on separate paper.

- Identify the significant accomplishments of the individual.

- Describe the conditions in American society the individual had to overcome.

- Explain how the individual's actions demonstrate self-determination.

Student Traveler

In small groups, research the historic sites in Washington, D.C. Then use your findings to respond to the following questions. Use your answers to create a travelogue describing each site, its historical significance, and the individual accomplishments it represents.

Benjamin Bannaker assisted in designing our nation's capital, Washington, D.C. Work cooperatively with classmates to plan a trip to our nation's capital to visit historical sites that document the accomplishments of African Americans such as Benjamin Bannaker. Use the Internet and reference materials to identify the places you will visit. Then answer the following questions about your trip.

1. How far is it from your home to Washington, D.C.? _____

2. How will you travel to Washington, D.C.? _____

3. Name four historic sites you plan to visit in the capital. Identify the historical significance of each location.

   1. _____

   2. _____

   3. _____

   4. _____

African American Cultural Themes

In Chapter 18, page 176, the author states: "Despite their tenuous hold on freedom and the laws stacked against them, Africans in America always looked for a better way of doing things—even as far back as Revolutionary times." Working in a small group, develop a creative display of African American inventors. Entitle your display: *19th Century African American Inventors and Innovators*. In the space provided, write a summary for the display. Focus on the spirit and resilience of these inventors as creative, accomplished, and productive men and women who worked during the 19th century without full citizenship rights in the country of their birth.

Africans in America during the 18th and 19th centuries were not legally enslaved; however, they were forced to live under oppressive and unjust conditions without full citizenship rights. Unit 6 highlights five of the nine African American cultural themes that helped them to endure these conditions.

- **Resilience**
- **Personal Style and Uniqueness**
- **Realness**
- **Communalism**
- **Humanism**

Refer to page viii for a description of these themes.

In Unit 6, the author celebrates the spirit of these Africans by calling it "indomitable" (p. 172) and "invincible" (p. 174), and shows how that spirit allowed Africans to remain undefeated and motivated (resilience). This unit also demonstrates the creativity (personal style and uniqueness) and activism (realness) that Africans displayed under oppressive conditions. The constant demands by free Africans for rights—not only for themselves but also for all Africans—provides yet another example of that invincible and indomitable spirit (communalism and humanism).

19th Century African American Inventors and Innovators

_____

_____

_____

_____

_____

_____

_____

_____

_____

_____

_____

_____

Note-taking Tips | PREWRITING

Write your notes in outline form in your own words. Keep a bibliography that includes the title of your sources, the name of each author, the date of publication, and the page numbers where you gathered information.

Ideas:

While taking notes, you do not need to write in complete sentences, but the ideas you write down should be complete enough to make sense of later.

Details:

Note the circumstances of this person's early life and childhood.

Details:

Note the key decisions and actions that led to this person's outstanding career.

Details:

Note the significant contributions of this person.

Choose a person from this unit whom you would like to know better. Research the life of that person to find out more about him or her. Take notes to prepare for writing a biographical sketch of this person's life.

Date: _____ Name of person chosen for a biographical sketch:

_____ _____

Title of source used: _____

Author: _____

Publisher: _____

Copyright Date: _____ Pages: _____

Ideas: _____

_____

_____

_____

_____

Birth and early life: _____

_____

_____

_____

_____

Decisions; turning points in the person's life: _____

_____

_____

_____

_____

Significant contributions: _____

_____

_____

_____

_____

Drafting Tips	**DRAFTING**

Begin with a prewriting activity such as a concept map or Venn diagram.

Use your notes on page 37 to help you draft your biographical sketch on a character chosen from the textbook. Remember to focus on the important events in the person's life, including national or international contributions.

Introductory Paragraph:

Try to find an important or interesting detail, idea, or fact about the person to open the sketch.

Introductory paragraph: _____

_____

_____

_____

_____

_____

Birth and Early Life:

What significant events helped to shape the "mind and heart" of this person in a unique way?

Birth and early life: _____

_____

_____

_____

_____

Main Contributions:

Focus on the big picture. What were the main turning points in this person's life? What made this individual unique? What motivated this individual? What contributions did this person make to society?

Main contributions: _____

_____

_____

_____

_____

_____

Conclusion:

Refer to the idea introduced in the opening paragraph. Why is this person's life story still significant today? What lasting contributions did he or she make?

Conclusion: _____

_____

_____

_____

_____

_____

Revising and Proofreading Tips

REVISING AND PROOFREADING

Polish and clean up your writing as you prepare for publication.

Read your biographical sketch aloud to determine whether it is clear and makes sense. As you read, mark the sentences that can be improved. Check to see whether you have used all the important information from your notes. Revise your sketch on the lines below.

Organization:

Check to make sure you have written a well-organized sketch that includes an introduction, several supporting paragraphs, and a conclusion.

Edit:

Anything in your sketch that does not add to your topic and main ideas should be removed.

Sentence Length:

Use some shorter, simple sentences between complex and compound ones.

Word Choice:

Have you used the best words to convey your meaning? Focus on choosing the best possible verbs and adjectives.

Check Your Style:

Fix any sentences that are choppy or awkward.

Proofread:

Check for problems with grammar, usage, punctuation, capitalization, and spelling.

Publishing Tips

PUBLISHING

Prepare your biographical sketch for publication.

Copy the clean, final biographical sketch on the lines below. With your teacher's help, decide how you want to "publish" your sketch. You may want to read it to your class, create a class scrapbook or writing portfolio, or post it on the bulletin board for others to read.

Visual Appeal:

Check your finished product to make sure it is visually appealing. The margins should be uniform and the lines evenly spaced. If you want to post your biographical sketch, it should be written in clear, bold letters. Use a dark ink pen, rather than pencil or red pen. Make sure the title is in large print so that it stands out.

Adding Graphics:

If an illustration or photograph of the person is available from the textbook or other source, consider copying it to include with your sketch. You may want to enlarge the image, as most copy machines have an enlargement feature. If you like to draw, think about creating your own "copy" of the illustration or photograph with an original drawing.

Visual Literacy

Review the painting on the Unit 7 Opener pages and on page 210 of your textbook. Which key idea does it reinforce? Write a caption that links this image to the unit title and the key idea in this unit.

Caption: _____

_____

_____

_____

Historical Context

Using information from the textbook, images and captions in Chapters 20–23 and Journey pages B3–B8, write an essay based on the bulleted items.

Compose your essay on separate paper.

- Discuss several ways in which Africans contested enslavement.
- Identify Africans who offered leadership during this difficult period.
- Compare the effectiveness of each approach.

Student Traveler

You are a filmmaker, and you have been asked to create a film about some historical sites that document the escape of Africans from American enslavement. The name of this film will be *Escaping Enslavement: Historical Sites*.

After reading Chapters 20 and 22 of your textbook, decide which historical sites you would like to film. Because of budget considerations, your film crew can visit only one location outside the United States and no more than four locations within the U.S. You must decide whether to send a crew to Haiti, Liberia, or Sierra Leone. Within the United States, you can choose to film in cities where volunteers supported the Underground Railroad. Begin your plan for filming by answering the following questions:

1. How will you treat the controversy over colonization?

_____

_____

2. What foreign location would offer the most interesting video presentation for viewers? _____

_____

3. How would you obtain information on the Underground Railroad? _____

_____

4. What sites in the United States will you include in the film? Why? _____

_____

African American Cultural Themes

Working in a small group, prepare a three-page booklet describing the oratorical style of three African abolitionists featured in Chapter 21 of your textbook. Using the textbook and other references, select at least one quotation per orator from a speech they have given. Then identify and explain the African American cultural themes represented in the quotes you have selected. Use the space below to plan your booklet.

Create your booklet on separate paper.

African abolitionists worked toward gaining their natural rights of freedom and justice. Unit 7 highlights eight of the nine African American cultural themes.

- **Realness**
- **Orality and Verbal Expressiveness**
- **Personal Style and Uniqueness**
- **Spirituality**
- **Communalism**
- **Humanism**
- **Resilience**
- **Emotional Vitality**

Refer to page viii for a description of these themes.

In Unit 7, the author describes how Africans who spoke out against the denial of their natural rights (realness) used the African oral tradition in distinctive ways to educate, persuade and motivate others (orality and verbal expressiveness, personal style and uniqueness). Their speeches and activities reveal an enduring belief in a higher power and a universal order (spirituality). Whether they were contesting enslavement, guiding runaway Africans to freedom, or advocating women's rights, their work was a collective effort to improve the quality of life of the oppressed (communalism and humanism). Their refusal to give up was fueled by a steadfast passion for their cause (resilience, emotional vitality).

Orator	Quote	Cultural Themes

Part A
Answering Document-Based Questions

**Document-Based
Questions test your
ability to analyze a
group of documents.**

Source:
Think about the
people who created
the document. What
was their goal?

Time of Origin:
What date marks
the creation of the
document? Think
about the event(s) that
prompted the creation
of the document.

Point of View:
What point of view
did the person who
produced the document
have? Consider the
document's source
and the time of origin
as you answer this.

Word Choice:
Focus on how the
choice of words
expresses the writer's
attitude toward the
subject and toward
the person being
addressed. Is the tone
serious, humorous,
sarcastic, or solemn?

**Review this unit about Africans' fight for freedom. Consider what it might have
been like to hear that you are now "free" after the Civil War.**

Directions: The following questions are based on primary sources in Unit 8. Review each
source and answer the questions that follow.

Document #1: Analyzing a Public Notice (Page 231)
Review the public meeting notice in Chapter 24 of your textbook.

1. Do you believe that this meeting is being held by supporters or by
   opponents of the Supreme Court decision? Give reasons to support
   your answer.

   _____

   _____

2. The notice says the meeting is to "consider the atrocious decision of
   the Supreme Court in the Dred Scott Case." What other purpose do
   you suppose the meeting could have?

   _____

   _____

   _____

Document #2: Analyzing a Letter (Page 249)
**Read the 19th century letter from Jourdon Anderson to Colonel P.H. Anderson
in Chapter 26 of your textbook. Note the date of the letter and the phrase "we
have concluded to test your sincerity by asking you to send us our wages for the
time we served you."**

1. Do you think that Jourdon Anderson really believed that Colonel
   Anderson would pay him all his back wages? Why or why not?

   _____

   _____

2. The postscript to the letter says "Say howdy to George Carter, and
   thank him for taking the pistol from you when you were shooting
   at me." How do these words indicate the attitude of the writer toward
   Colonel Anderson?

   _____

   _____

Part B
Drafting a Document-Based Essay

Drafting Tips

Begin with a prewriting activity such as a concept map or Venn diagram.

Historical Context: Africans who lived during the period of the Dred Scott Decision, and who survived the Civil War, had first-hand experience with the meaning of freedom. The escape from the despair of the 1850s and the emerging opportunities of the mid-1860s must have sparked new hopes for a better life among the newly freed Africans.

Task: Using information from Documents 1 and 2 and your knowledge of African American history, write an essay in which you discuss:

Analysis:

Think about the similarities and differences between the documents.

- the reaction of free Africans to the Dred Scott Decision.

- the sense of empowerment that freedom brought to Jourdon Anderson and other free Africans.

- the kinds of choices that Africans would assume they had after 1865.

- the realities that free Africans faced in the South and the North.

Thesis Statement:

Write a thesis statement that identifies the topic of your essay. Be careful not to simply restate the topic.

Thesis Statement: _____

_____

_____

_____

_____

Supporting Ideas:

Generate a list of details that support your thesis statement. Use a quote or other specific details from a document to support your thesis statement.

Supporting Ideas: _____

_____

_____

_____

_____

_____

_____

Conclusion:

End your essay with a concluding paragraph that restates or sums up your main ideas.

Conclusion: _____

_____

_____

_____

_____

_____

Revising and Proofreading Tips

REVISING AND PROOFREADING

Polish and clean up your writing as you prepare for publication.

Read your essay aloud to determine whether it is clear and makes sense. As you read, mark the sentences that can be improved. Make sure you have used all the important information from your notes. Revise your essay on the lines below.

Organization:

Check to make sure you have written a well-organized essay that includes an introduction, several supporting paragraphs, and a conclusion.

Edit:

Delete anything in your essay that does not add to your thesis or supporting ideas.

Sentence Length:

Use some shorter, simple sentences between complex and compound ones.

Word Choice:

Have you used the best words to convey your meaning? Focus on choosing the best possible verbs and adjectives.

Check Your Style:

Fix any sentences that are choppy or awkward.

Proofread:

Check for problems with grammar, usage, punctuation, capitalization, and spelling.

_____

_____

_____

_____

_____

_____

_____

_____

_____

_____

_____

_____

_____

_____

_____

_____

_____

_____

_____

_____

_____

_____

_____

_____

_____

_____

PUBLISHING

Prepare your essay for publication.

Copy the clean, final version of your essay on the lines below and add a title. With your teacher's help, decide how you want to "publish" your essay. You may want to post it on the classroom bulletin board, make a class scrapbook or writing portfolio, or read it to the class.

Visual Appeal:

Check your finished product to make sure it is visually appealing. The margins should be uniform and the lines evenly spaced. If you want to post your essay, it should be written in clear, bold letters. Use a dark ink pen, rather than pencil or red pen. Make sure the title is in large print so that it stands out.

Adding Graphics:

Consider adding a graphic—such as a photograph, an illustration, or a map—to enhance the "look" of your final product.

Visual Literacy

Review the images on pages B1–B8. Then answer the following questions.

1. Why do you think the author chose the title "Journey" to describe these 15 color images? _____

_____

2. What is the relationship between the images on pages B1 and B2? How are these images similar, and different, from the others in the Journey color visuals? _____

_____

_____

Historical Context

Using information from the textbook and the Journey color visuals on pages B1–B8, write an essay based on the bulleted items.

Compose your essay on separate paper.

- Identify some of the major African American contributions to the field of art.

- Analyze individual art pieces. Choose one African artifact from B1–B2, two paintings from B3–B7, and one sculpture from B8.

- Discuss the journey that these art selections symbolize and make a connection that shows a relationship between them.

Student Traveler

Imagine that you and a group of students are driving to Washington, D.C. to visit some African American historical sites, including the Library of Congress, where you will view the draft of the Emancipation Proclamation. Work in small groups to complete the following exercises in preparation for your trip.

1. On a classroom map of the United States, use string to connect the location of your hometown to Washington, D.C. Label the two cities and write the miles and kilometers between your hometown and the nation's capital.

   Miles: _____   Kilometers: _____

2. Using the classroom map and a detailed road map, chart your route and answer these questions:

   a. What major cities and states will you pass through?

   _____

   b. About how many total miles will you travel?

   _____

3. If your car gets 35 miles to the gallon, how much gasoline will you need? _____

African American Cultural Themes

Working in a small group or with another student, review the two quotations by Colonel Higginson in Chapter 26 (p. 246) regarding the courage of African soldiers.

Write at least five points that argue against the following erroneous statement: African soldiers did not make a contribution to the war and were not organized, competent, or courageous. Use Higginson's quotes as part of your argument. Include a discussion of how the courage of African soldiers flowed from principles and themes in their culture. Use the space provided to organize your thoughts.

Write your position statement on separate paper.

In Unit 8, the courage and spirit of African soldiers is celebrated. Their actions highlight four of the nine African American cultural themes:

- **Humanism**—a concern for human beings, their condition, interests, and achievements
- **Communalism**—a sense of community; a coming together of a people
- **Resilience**—the ability to bounce back from disappointment, oppression, and disaster to renew life's energy and continue forward
- **Emotional Vitality**—an expression of liveliness and openness conveyed in the language, oral literature, song, dance, body language, and folk poetry of a people

Once again, African soldiers fought in a war for the freedom of others, before they had citizenship rights for themselves (humanism). The segregated units of soldiers distinguished themselves as brave and accomplished men with an inner strength that kept their commitment steady, and their hope for freedom alive (communalism and resilience). When the Emancipation Proclamation was ratified, and the Civil War ended, Africans were overjoyed. The author describes their emotional response to the news that they were finally free (emotional vitality).

Cultural Themes	Supporting Examples
Humanism	
Communalism	
Resilience	
Emotional Vitality	

Note-taking Tips | PREWRITING

Read the account of *Plessy v. Ferguson* on page 275 of your textbook again and record information and details to support your answers. You may also need to conduct additional research. Include the title, author's name, publisher, copyright date, and page references of your source(s).

Indicate:

In your notes, indicate why Homer Plessy was arrested.

Explain:

Explain why this case made it to the Supreme Court.

Note:

Note why the Supreme Court denied Plessy his rights.

Describe:

Describe Harlan's response to this decision.

Record:

Record the effects of this decision.

Review this unit about the Reconstruction years. Read the Multiple Perspectives feature in Chapter 29, After You Read (p. 277). Use the questions below to help you organize an editorial about the *Plessy* v. *Ferguson* case.

State the main idea of the editorial: _____

_____

What was the issue in the case of *Plessy* v. *Ferguson*? _____

_____

_____

_____

What was the majority opinion of the Court? _____

_____

_____

_____

What stands out about the written position of the Supreme Court Justice you have selected to compare with Judge Harlan? _____

_____

_____

_____

What did Judge Harlan say was his reason for dissenting in this case?

_____

_____

_____

Do you agree or disagree with Harlan's position? _____

_____

_____

_____

Drafting Tips

DRAFTING

Begin with a prewriting activity such as a concept map or Venn diagram.

Use your notes from the previous page to help you draft your editorial. Remember to include enough interesting and informative details to make the audience feel as if they have actually met the individual. Use these questions to help organize your thoughts: What is the issue and what are the main points you want to make? How did this case affect African Americans? Was Harlan's decision justified?

Introductory Paragraph:

This paragraph should explain the issue in the case of *Plessy* v. *Ferguson*.

Introductory Paragraph: _____

_____

_____

_____

_____

_____

Opposing Positions:

This paragraph should compare the position of the selected Supreme Court Justice with that of Judge Harlan.

Opposing Positions: _____

_____

_____

_____

_____

_____

Effects:

This paragraph should relate the effects of the Supreme Court's decision.

The effects of the decision: _____

_____

_____

_____

_____

Conclusion:

Assess Harlan's dissent. Do you agree or disagree with it? Is history on your side?

Harlan's dissent then and now: _____

_____

_____

_____

_____

_____

_____

Revising and Proofreading Tips

REVISING AND PROOFREADING

Polish and clean up your writing as you prepare for publication.

When you revise your editorial, make sure that you have included all the main points and supporting details that describe your issue. Review your notes to make sure that you have not omitted any important information. Revise your editorial on the lines below.

Organization:

Check to make sure you have written a well-organized editorial that includes an introductory paragraph, supporting paragraphs, and a conclusion.

Edit:

Anything in your editorial that does not add to your topic and main ideas should be removed.

Sentence Length:

Use some shorter, simple sentences between complex and compound ones.

Word Choice:

Have you used the best words to convey your meaning? Focus on choosing the best possible verbs and adjectives.

Check Your Style:

Fix any sentences that are choppy or awkward.

Proofread:

Check for problems with grammar, usage, punctuation, capitalization, and spelling.

_____

_____

_____

_____

_____

_____

_____

_____

_____

_____

_____

_____

_____

_____

_____

_____

_____

_____

_____

_____

_____

_____

_____

_____

_____

_____

_____

_____

Publishing Tips

PUBLISHING

Prepare your editorial for publication.

Copy the clean, final version of your editorial on the lines below. With your teacher's help, decide how you want to "publish" your editorial. You may want to read it to your class, add it to your scrapbook or writing portfolio, or post it on the bulletin board for others to read.

Visual Appeal:

Check your finished product to make sure it is visually appealing. The margins should be uniform and the lines evenly spaced. If you want to post your editorial, it should be written in clear, bold letters. Use a dark ink pen, rather than pencil or red pen. Make sure the title is in large print so that it stands out.

Adding Graphics:

Consider adding a graphic—such as a photograph, an illustration, or a map—to enhance the "look" of your final product.

Visual Literacy

Review the key ideas presented in the Unit 9 Summary. Then look at the photographs on pages 263, 266, and 279. What four important challenges do these photographs represent to African Americans after the Civil War? On the lines provided, express each of these challenges as depicted by the photographs.

1. _____

2. _____

3. _____

4. _____

Historical Context

Using information from the text and the letter on page 273, write an essay based on the bulleted items.

Compose your essay on separate paper.

- Identify specific acts of violence directed at African Americans in the South during Reconstruction.

- Discuss causes of that violence.

- Compare the treatment of Africans in the North and South during and after Reconstruction.

Student Traveler

In small groups, research the Old West. Then use your findings to respond to the following questions. On separate paper create a map of the Old West. Include locations and interesting geographical information from your research.

Chapter 30 ends with an account of the legendary African American, Nat Love, sometimes known as Deadwood Dick. An outstanding cowboy, Love became a hero to many African Americans who read about life in the Wild West and may have enticed those who wanted to go there. Perhaps they would have had the good fortune of riding with stagecoach driver Mary Fields, one of the few African cowgirls.

1. What did your group find most interesting about the history of the Old West? _____

2. What are some of the legends of the period that you discovered? _____

   _____

3. Would you have liked to live in the West at that time? Why or why not? _____

   _____

4. How did you find your information? _____

   _____

African American Cultural Themes

On page 281 of your textbook the author writes: "But African Americans would continue the pattern of resiliency, courage against the odds, and perseverance that began in the Middle Passage."

Working with a partner, discuss this statement and decide on three significant examples of resilience and courage among African people as they struggled against racism during the period before the Civil War. Write these in an essay entitled: "Courage Against the Odds." Use the space provided to plan your essay.

After the Civil War ended, African Americans were free but unable to provide themselves with basic life needs. This unit highlights two of the nine African American cultural themes that helped the newly freed Africans to survive these new challenges.

- **Communalism**—a sense of community; a coming together of a people
- **Resilience**—the ability to bounce back from disappointment, oppression and disaster and to renew life's energy and continue forward

In this unit, African Americans came together to form labor unions, build schools, and elect public officials (communalism). They did this while having to protect each other from brutal and racist violence by whites—even as they experienced the failure of Reconstruction to grant them full rights of citizenship (resilience).

Courage Against the Odds

Note-taking Tips | PREWRITING

Use the following tips to plan your play.

Research:

Read the textbook pages noted in parentheses for each question. Then answer the questions in your own words.

Characters:

To develop your characters, include the name, age, gender, interests, physical characteristics, and occupation of each.

Setting:

Identify the time (year) and place (the name of a city) of the meeting and some details about the surroundings.

Plot:

Describe how the characters meet and what actions may come out of their meeting.

Review this unit about the African American migration. Write a one-act play featuring a meeting of two African Americans: a person who migrated from the South and a northern worker.

Title of the Play: _____

Using your textbook, find information about the migration of African Americans to the North. The following questions will help guide your research.

1. What political right was denied African Americans in the South? (pp. 311–312)

_____

_____

2. What actions did southern whites take to further the segregation of African Americans? (pp. 320–321)

_____

_____

3. What other factors accelerated the migration of African Americans to northern cities? (pp. 322–323)

_____

_____

4. How were African Americans received in the North, and what challenges did they face in northern society? (pp. 324–325)

_____

_____

Create two characters: one from the North and one from the South. In the space provided, list details for the characters, setting, and plot.

Northern Worker (NW): _____

_____

Southern Migrant (SM): _____

_____

Setting: _____

Plot: _____

_____

Drafting Tips

DRAFTING

Use your notes to prepare your first draft.

Use your notes to help draft your script for a one-act play. Include the name of each character in the space provided; note that NW stands for Northern Worker and SM stands for Southern Migrant.

Narrator:

The narrator opens the play with a description of the setting and the characters. He or she introduces the characters by name and age, and briefly describes their occupations and the general circumstances of their meeting.

Characters:

Have the characters respond to one another in a friendly, conversational manner.

Narrator:
(name)
_____
_____
_____

NW:
(name)
_____
_____

NW:
(name)
_____
_____

SM:
(name)
_____
_____

SM:
(name)
_____
_____

NW:
(name)
_____
_____

NW:
(name)
_____
_____

SM:
(name)
_____
_____

SM:
(name)
_____
_____

NW:
(name)
_____
_____

NW:
(name)
_____
_____

Revising and Proofreading Tips

REVISING AND PROOFREADING

Polish and clean up your writing as you prepare for publication.

This step is important for producing a believable script. Check to see whether you have used all the important information from the Prewriting section. Revise your script on the lines below.

Organization:

Check to make sure the details in the play are introduced in a way that makes sense.

Read:

Read the script aloud to make sure it flows smoothly. Do your characters sound like real people? As you read, mark the sections of dialogue that can be improved.

Edit:

Any dialogue or background information that does not sound real, or does not fit into the historical context of the play, should be replaced or removed.

Word Choice:

Focus on how your choice of words expresses your characters' attitude. Have you used the best possible verbs and adjectives in your script to make the dialogue come alive?

Proofread:

Check for problems with grammar, usage, punctuation, capitalization, and spelling.

_____
_____
_____
_____
_____
_____
_____
_____
_____
_____
_____
_____
_____
_____
_____
_____
_____
_____
_____
_____
_____
_____
_____
_____
_____
_____
_____
_____
_____
_____

| *Publishing Tips* | **PUBLISHING** |

Prepare your play for presentation.

Copy the clean, final version of your script on the lines below. With your teacher's help, decide how you want to "publish" your script. You may want to post it on the classroom bulletin board, add it to your class scrapbook or writing portfolio, or act it out for the class.

Visual Appeal:

Check your finished product to make sure it is visually appealing. The margins should be uniform and the lines evenly spaced. If you want to post your play, it should be written in clear, bold letters. Use a dark ink pen, rather than pencil or red pen. Make sure the title is in large print so that it stands out.

Rehearse:

Be sure to rehearse your play several times before you present it to your class. As you rehearse, think about the circumstances of your characters' lives and the feelings behind their words. The way you present yourself "on stage" will show your audience how those circumstances have affected them in the past and present.

Visual Literacy

Review the images in the New Horizons color visuals on pages C1–C8. Then answer the following questions.

1. Compare and contrast *From Slavery to Reconstruction* with *Black Manhattan*. How does the image of the city in the mural differ from the one in the collage? _____

_____

_____

2. Look at *War Knows No Color Line* on page C3 and read the caption. How do you think the artist felt about Africans participating in World War I? _____

_____

_____

Historical Context

Unit 10 includes several African American leaders who emerged at the turn of the century. Study the paintings and read the captions on pages C8 and C4. Then write an essay based on the bulleted items entitled "Ancestors Carved in Stone."

Compose your essay on separate paper.

• Explain the similarities between these two paintings.

• Show how both paintings represent upward mobility for all African Americans.

Student Traveler

In small groups, research the migration of southern African Americans to the North. Try to put yourself in their position and imagine what this decision would be like for you and your family. Answer the questions in the space provided. Use your answers to develop the first chapter of your oral family history entitled "Leaving Home, Coming Home."

Chapter 34 relates the great migration of Africans from the South to the North. Imagine that you are an African American who wants to remind your family of your own migration to the North by telling it to them as a family history.

1. What was your life like in the South? _____

_____

2. Why did you leave the South? Did you travel alone or with others? _____

_____

3. Where did you settle in the North? Was it difficult to find a job? Did you make friends? _____

_____

African American Cultural Themes

Review the description of the work of Ida B. Wells and William Monroe Trotter on pages 301–303. Working with a small group, create a script for a short one-act play that features a discussion between Wells and Trotter, comparing their style of advocacy and activism with Booker T. Washington's policy of accommodation. Use the space provided to plan your play.

You may use the blank pages at the back of the Worktext if you need additional space.

By the turn of the century, the resilience of African Americans had been continually tested. To many, it seemed that white oppression and violence against African Americans would never end. This unit highlights seven of the nine African American Cultural themes:

- **Orality and Verbal Expressiveness**
- **Emotional Vitality**
- **Personal Style and Uniqueness**
- **Communalism**
- **Humanism**
- **Spirituality**

Refer to page viii for a description of these themes.

In Unit 10, a group of bold, fiery leaders forcefully protested white oppression and violence (orality and verbal expressiveness, emotional vitality, and personal style and uniqueness). Their demands for freedom and justice were greatly influenced by their cultural traditions as they worked with others for the good of the community (communalism) and fearlessly confronted the attempts of whites to dehumanize their people. This willingness to give of oneself, despite oppression (humanism), and the belief in the ultimate goodness of all people (spirituality) are recurring themes in the history of African American people.

ACT I

Title: _____

Setting: _____

Scene: _____

Wells: _____

Trotter: _____

Wells: _____

Trotter: _____

Part A
Answering Document-Based Questions

Note-taking Tips

Document-Based Questions test your ability to analyze a group of documents.

Word Choice:

Focus on how the choice of words expresses the writer's attitude toward the subject.

Inferences:

Look for key words in the document to support your conclusions.

Analyze:

A photograph captures a moment in time and can be a powerful communication tool. Pay close attention to details such as facial expression, body language, and setting. Reflect on the messages these details send to an observer.

Review this unit about African agency in the early 1900s. All across the globe, people of African descent demonstrated a belief in self-determination and self-improvement.

Directions: The following questions are based on documents in Unit 11 that reflect a vision of self-determination and self-improvement for people of African descent. Review each document and answer the questions that follow.

Document #1: Analyzing a Literary Quote (Page 329)
Review the quote on the opening pages for Unit 11, then answer the questions that follow.

1. How do Garvey's words demonstrate agency?

   _____

   _____

2. How did Garvey craft his words so that white listeners would not be threatened by his determination?

   _____

   _____

3. What does the carefully constructed message indicate about Garvey's leadership skills?

   _____

   _____

Document #2: Analyzing a Photo and Caption (Page 372)
Review the photo of Mary McLeod Bethune and students, then read the caption beneath the photo to answer the following questions.

1. What message do you receive from the non-verbal communication you observe in the photo?

   _____

   _____

2. How did the actions of Mary McLeod Bethune demonstrate agency?

   _____

   _____

Drafting Tips	**Part B** **Drafting A Document-Based Essay**

Begin with a prewriting activity such as a concept map or Venn diagram.

Historical Context: During the first half of the 20th century, African Americans embraced the ideas of self-determination and self-improvement. They sought to express their uniqueness without the burden of shame or fear.

Analysis:

Think about the similarities and differences between the documents.

Task: **For most people, graduating from high school represents entry into the adult world. It is a time when each individual makes critical decisions about his or her life path. Reflect on the messages communicated from the documents from page 61. Write a well-organized essay in which you discuss:**

- **how each message delivered to members of the African American community over 70 years ago still applies to the students graduating from your school this year**

- **how you will incorporate the messages into your own life**

- **why self-improvement and self-determination should be primary goals for everyone**

Thesis Statement:

Write a thesis statement that identifies the topic of your essay. Be careful not to simply restate the topic.

Thesis Statement: _____

_____

_____

_____

_____

Supporting Ideas:

Generate a list of details that support your thesis statement. Use a quote or other specific details from a document to support your thesis statement.

Supporting Ideas: _____

_____

_____

_____

_____

_____

Conclusion:

End your essay with a concluding paragraph that restates or sums up your main ideas.

Conclusion: _____

_____

_____

_____

_____

_____

Revising and Proofreading Tips

REVISING AND PROOFREADING

Polish and clean up your writing as you prepare for publication.

When revising your essay, make sure each part of the topic has been covered. Review your essay to ensure that you have addressed each point.

Organization:

Check to make sure you have written a well-organized essay that includes an introduction, several supporting paragraphs, and a conclusion.

Edit:

Delete anything in your essay that does not add to your thesis and supporting ideas.

Sentence Length:

Use some shorter, simple sentences between complex and compound ones.

Word Choice:

Have you used the best words to convey your meaning? Focus on choosing the best possible verbs and adjectives.

Check Your Style:

Fix any sentences that are choppy or awkward.

Proofread:

Check for problems with grammar, usage, punctuation, capitalization, and spelling.

_____
_____
_____
_____
_____
_____
_____
_____
_____
_____
_____
_____
_____
_____
_____
_____
_____
_____
_____
_____
_____
_____
_____
_____
_____
_____
_____

Publishing Tips

PUBLISHING

Prepare your essay for publication.

Copy the clean, final version of your essay on the lines below and add a title. With your teacher's help, decide how you want to "publish" your essay. You may want to post it on the classroom bulletin board, make a class scrapbook, read your essay to the class, or add it to your writing portfolio.

Visual Appeal:

Check your finished product to make sure it is visually appealing. The margins should be uniform and the lines evenly spaced. If you want to post your essay, it should be written in clear, bold letters. Use a dark ink pen, rather than pencil or red pen. Make sure the title is in large print so that it stands out.

Adding Graphics:

Consider adding a graphic—such as a photograph, an illustration, or a map—to enhance the "look" of your final product.

Title: _____

_____

_____

_____

_____

_____

_____

_____

_____

_____

_____

_____

_____

_____

_____

_____

_____

_____

_____

_____

_____

_____

_____

_____

_____

Visual Literacy

Carefully observe the photograph found in the Unit Opener on page 330 and on page 347. What key idea does the photograph reinforce? On the lines provided, write a caption that links this image to the unit title and key idea of this unit.

Caption: _____

_____

_____

_____

Historical Context

Refer to the color visual titled *Migration of the Negro* by Jacob Lawrence, on page C2. Read the caption and describe what the panel depicts. Use this information and what you have learned from Unit 11 to compose an essay based on the bulleted items.

Compose your essay on separate paper.

- Explain how the panel could represent actions of the African American community during the early 1900s.

- Compare what the crowd depicted in the painting hoped to find with southerners who moved northward during the 1920s.

- Explain how the actions of both groups display agency.

Student Traveler

In Chapter 37, the author states that Marcus Garvey "was the spark that rekindled African Americans' appreciation for their history and culture." The headquarters of the Universal Negro Improvement Association (UNIA) was located in Harlem, New York. Write or call the Harlem Visitors and Convention Association and ask about historical sites, libraries, and museums, and for materials and information related to Marcus Garvey and the actions of the UNIA. Then work together in small groups to create an itinerary. Be sure to include a trip to the Schomburg Center of Research in Black Culture. The Schomburg Center houses collections of thousands of African American historical papers, books, and artifacts.

Use the street map of Harlem on page 359 of your textbook and information from the Harlem Visitors and Convention Association to answer the following questions:

1. Where are the following points of interest located?

   UNIA Headquarters _____

   Marcus Garvey's Home _____

   Schomburg Center _____

2. What three additional points of interest in Harlem would you like to visit? _____

   _____

3. What major U.S. cities will you pass through as you travel to Harlem? _____

   _____

4. Approximately how many total miles will you be traveling?

   _____

African American Cultural Themes

Working together in teams, find five examples of communalism in the acts and beliefs of African Americans in Unit 11.

Write a five-paragraph essay— one paragraph for each example of communalism. Entitle your essay "African American Communalism" or choose another title that summarizes the main ideas of the essay. Use the space provided to write your examples. Then list your reason for choosing each example.

You may use the blank pages at the back of the Worktext if you need additional space.

Unit 11 highlights all nine of the African American cultural themes:

- **Resilience**
- **Humanism**
- **Communalism**
- **Musicality/Rhythm**
- **Orality and Verbal Expressiveness**

- **Personal Style and Uniqueness**
- **Realness**
- **Spirituality**
- **Emotional Vitality**

Refer to page viii for a description of these themes.

Unit 11 tells the story of African American soldiers during World War I who fought for their country in segregated units (resilience, humanism, communalism). These men risked their lives and some even gave their lives to fight for the rights of others— rights that they were denied at home. Pan-Africanism took hold and Marcus Garvey's movement gained momentum with calls for African pride and a focus on collective economics (communalism). The creative artists of the Harlem Renaissance expressed many of the cultural themes in their work (musicality/ rhythm, orality and verbal expressiveness, personal style and uniqueness, realness, spirituality, emotional vitality). African Americans were willing to be blacklisted by the government because they dared to examine communism as a way to provide a better life for their people (resilience). Finally, African Americans looked to one another for support as a way to survive the ravages of the Great Depression (communalism).

Examples of African Amerian Communalism	Supporting Reasons
1. _____	
2. _____	
3. _____	
4. _____	
5. _____	

Note-taking Tips | PREWRITING

Write your notes in outline form in your own words.

Review this unit about the progress of African Americans during the middle of the 20th century and write a campaign speech for Adam Clayton Powell, Jr., as a candidate for president of the United States in 1968. Gather information from the textbook and other resources. Include the answers to the following questions in your notes.

Paraphrase:

While taking notes, you do not need to write in complete sentences, but the information you write down should be complete enough to make sense later.

Explore Your Topics:

During your research, gather as much information about the candidate as you can.

Make Your Case:

Each fact should clearly and convincingly communicate why the candidate is the best person for the job.

Word Choice:

Think about how the words you choose define your tone, which can be serious, humorous, sarcastic, solemn, etc. Reflect on the message a listener will receive based on the words you select.

Title of Speech: _____

1. What was Powell's education and early training in political action? (pages 385–386) _____

    _____

2. What were Powell's previously held elective offices? (page 386)

    _____

    _____

3. What is Powell's record as a leader in Congress? (page 387)

    _____

    _____

4. How would you describe Powell as a political thinker? (page 386)

    _____

    _____

    _____

5. How did Powell handle political controversy? (page 387)

    _____

    _____

    _____

6. What personal qualities would make Powell an effective president? (pages 386–387) _____

    _____

Drafting Tips

Use your notes to prepare the first draft.

DRAFTING

Use the answers to the previous questions to help you draft the campaign speech. You may want to read a famous speech, such as Dr. Martin Luther King's "I Have a Dream," before you begin to write.

Introduction:

Begin your speech by enthusiastically greeting the audience. Then, the first paragraph of your speech should clearly and concisely communicate the positions of the candidate.

Introduction: _____

_____

_____

_____

_____

_____

_____

Supporting Paragraphs:

Each supporting paragraph should introduce one of your topics. The remaining sentences should provide supporting details about this topic. These sentences should explain how the candidate's experiences have prepared him for political office.

Supporting Paragraphs: _____

_____

_____

_____

_____

_____

_____

Language:

Use plain and simple language, as if you were talking to a friend.

_____

_____

_____

_____

_____

Conclusion:

Make sure your speech ends with a concise, but strong, restatement of the candidate's positions.

Conclusion: _____

_____

_____

_____

_____

_____

_____

Revising and Proofreading Tips

REVISING AND PROOFREADING

Polish and clean up your speech as you prepare for delivery.

This step is important in producing a dynamic speech. Read the speech aloud to hear how it sounds. The cadence or rhythm of the speech is important. Good speakers know where to pause and where to raise their voices. The speech should include some good "sound bites," or short, dramatic statements. Revise your speech on the lines below.

Organization:

Check to make sure you have written a well-organized speech that includes an introduction, several supporting paragraphs, and a conclusion.

Edit:

Anything in your speech that does not add to your topics and main ideas should be removed.

Sentence Length:

Use some shorter, simple sentences between complex and compound ones.

Word Choice:

Have you used the best words to convey your meaning? Focus on choosing the best possible verbs and adjectives.

Check Your Style:

Fix any sentences that are choppy or awkward.

Proofread:

Check for problems with grammar, usage, punctuation, capitalization, and spelling.

Delivering the Speech

Prepare to deliver your speech to an audience.

Practice Your Delivery:

Practice delivering your speech at home in a quiet place. You may even want to practice in front of friends or family members.

Style:

Use dramatic pauses to highlight powerful sentences in your speech.

Tone:

To keep your audience interested, vary the pitch and tone of your voice.

Audience:

As much as possible, keep your eyes focused on the audience to hold their attention. If you practiced delivering your speech, you may have memorized parts of it. This will help you to get your eyes off the page.

Your Voice:

Speak clearly so that everyone in the audience can hear you.

Pace Yourself:

Relax and speak naturally. Do not speak too quickly or too slowly.

PUBLISHING

Copy a clean final version of your speech on the lines below. With your teacher's help, decide how you want to "publish" your speech. In addition to delivering it to the class, you may want to post it on the classroom bulletin board or add it to your scrapbook or writing portfolio.

_____

_____

_____

_____

_____

_____

_____

_____

_____

_____

_____

_____

_____

_____

_____

_____

_____

_____

_____

_____

_____

_____

_____

_____

Visual Literacy

In Unit 12 there are seven photographs of individual African Americans who have made significant contributions to African American history and culture. Review the photographs and note those individuals you already know about or are interested in learning more about. List each of the leaders and write a comment about each one.

	Leader	Comment
1.	_____	_____
2.	_____	_____
3.	_____	_____
4.	_____	_____
5.	_____	_____
6.	_____	_____
7.	_____	_____

Historical Context

Using information from the textbook and the photos on pages 394 and 395, write an essay based on the bulleted items.

Compose your essay on separate paper.

- What role did Eleanor Roosevelt play in establishing a flying school at the Tuskegee Institute in Alabama?

- How did the Tuskegee Airmen distinguish themselves in service to their country during World War II?

- What effect did their accomplishments have on the recruitment of African American pilots and the desegregation of the armed forces?

Student Traveler

Use the information from your research to answer the questions.

Then, create an outline map of Europe during World War II to show the operating strategy of the Red Ball Express. On your map: locate the approximate position where the Red Ball Express was based; indicate the position of the armies advancing on Europe and the landing at Normandy; show one possible route for the Red Ball Express.

Construct your map on separate paper.

Chapter 42 relates the experience of African Americans who served as members of the Red Ball Express in World War II. Using the textbook and other resources, find out more about the Red Ball Express and the African Americans who delivered supplies to the army as it advanced toward Germany.

1. Where was the Red Ball Express based? _____

_____

2. Where did the Red Ball Express operate? _____

_____

3. What role did the Red Ball Express play in the allied invasion of Normandy? _____

African American Cultural Themes

Working in small groups, choose five of eight African American Cultural Themes highlighted in Unit 12.

Write and illustrate an example for each of the five cultural themes that you chose. Use the space provided to list each cultural theme with examples.

You may use the blank pages at the back of the Worktext if you need additional space.

Unit 12 highlights eight of the nine African American cultural themes:

- **Spirituality**
- **Resilience**
- **Emotional Vitality**
- **Humanism**
- **Personal Style and Uniqueness**
- **Communalism**
- **Orality and Verbal Expressiveness**
- **Realness**

Refer to page viii for a description of these themes.

In spite of tremendous obstacles, African Americans continued to show a firm resolve to reach greater levels of achievement (spirituality, resilience, emotional vitality). African American soldiers who showed great courage and skills were celebrated as heroes in the service of their country (humanism). African American scientists developed important new medical procedures that advanced the field of medicine worldwide. Gifted African American athletes broke new records and dominated their fields (emotional vitality, personal style and uniqueness). African American activists continued the struggle for justice and equality with protest marches, boycotts, and legal measures (communalism, orality and verbal expressiveness, realness) that sparked a social revolution.

Cultural Themes	Examples in African American Life

Note-taking Tips | PREWRITING

Research historical
accounts of the Freedom
Rides as you prepare to
write a news story, and
record your sources.

Pretend that you are a news reporter. The year is 1961 and your editor has assigned you to cover one of the Freedom Rides that are occurring throughout the South. As you prepare to write your news story, review this unit about the Freedom Movement and refer to the section on Freedom Rides on page 411. Also use a variety of other resources to find out more about the Freedom Rides. Use the following to help you plan your news story:

Ask Questions:

Focus on the six question words used by reporters—**who, what, where, when, why, and how**—to add details to your story.

1. In what city and state did the event occur? _____
   _____

2. Describe the event in your own words. _____
   _____
   _____

Analyze:

Interpret the impact of the event on society and the Civil Rights Movement based on your impressions and observations of the historical records.

3. Describe any acts of violence that you witnessed while covering the event. _____
   _____
   _____

4. What was most memorable about the event? _____
   _____
   _____

Quotes:

As you do your research, look for comments made by people who actually participated in the Freedom Rides—or opposed them—that you can turn into quotes for your story.

5. What were your impressions of the Freedom Riders? _____
   _____
   _____
   _____

6. What were your impressions of people opposed to the event? _____
   _____
   _____

7. Write a quote from one or more interesting persons that you "interviewed."_____
   _____
   _____
   _____

DRAFTING

Drafting Tips

Begin with your lead, followed by your facts and details presented in the order of most important to least important.

Use your notes from the Prewriting activity to help draft your news story. Your lead will probably be a compelling statement about a major act of violence or some other memorable feature of the event. Be sure that you present the most important information at the beginning of your story— the Who, What, When, Where, Why, and How. Background information and quotes should follow. Your conclusion should tie all of the details together and provide your interpretation of what the event means to society and to the African American struggle for civil rights.

Headline:

Write a headline that will grab a reader's attention.

Headline: _____

_____

_____

A Compelling Lead:

The lead of a news story is similar to a topic sentence or a thesis statement. It grabs the reader's attention by stating the main idea.

Lead: _____

_____

_____

_____

_____

Organization of Details:

Organize the information from your research. Focus on the six question words.

Details: _____

_____

_____

_____

_____

Quotes:

Most news stories use quotes to add interest and realism. Be sure to identify any source(s) that you quote.

Quotes: _____

_____

_____

_____

_____

Conclusion:

Your concluding paragraph should sum up the importance of the event.

Conclusion: _____

_____

_____

_____

_____

Revising and Proofreading Tips

REVISING AND PROOFREADING

Polish and clean up your writing as you prepare for publication.

When revising your news story, make sure that you have included all the main points, facts, and supporting details a reader would want to know. Review your notes from page 73, and the Organization of Details and Quotes sections from the previous page to make sure that you have not omitted any important information. Revise your news story on the lines below.

Headline: _____

Organization and Style:

Does your news story flow smoothly from one idea to the next? Read it aloud to make sure it "reads" well.

Edit:

Anything in your news story that does not add to your topic and supporting details should be removed.

Sentence Length:

Generally, news stories are made up of short sentences that mostly contain facts. This practice helps to keep readers interested and focused.

Word Choice:

Have you used the best words to convey your meaning? Focus on choosing the best possible verbs and adjectives.

Proofread:

Check for problems with grammar, usage, punctuation, capitalization, and spelling.

Publishing Tips

PUBLISHING

Prepare your news story for publication.

Copy the clean, final version of your news story on the lines below. With your teacher's help, decide how you want to "publish" your story. You may want to read it to your class, create a writing portfolio, make a class scrapbook entitled "Stories of the Freedom Riders," or post it on the classroom bulletin board for others to read.

Visual Appeal:

Check your finished product to make sure it is visually appealing. The margins should be uniform and the lines evenly spaced. If you want to post your news story, it should be written in clear, bold letters. Use a dark ink pen, rather than a pencil or red. Make sure the headline is in large print so that it stands out.

Adding Graphics:

Consider adding a graphic—such as a photograph, an illustration, or a map—to enhance the "look" of your final product.

Headline: _____

_____

_____

_____

_____

_____

_____

_____

_____

_____

_____

_____

_____

_____

_____

_____

_____

_____

_____

_____

Visual Literacy

In Unit 13, there are many photographs of African Americans organized to protest discrimination. Several different forms of protest are depicted. Review the photographs and note the methods of protest being used. Do you think that those protests were effective in achieving the objective that each group of protestors was seeking? Use the table provided to identify the method of protest, its goal, and your opinion about its effectiveness.

Photograph/Method of Protest	Goal/Effectiveness
1.	
2.	
3.	
4.	
5.	
6.	

Historical Context

Unit 13 discusses the theme of "The Freedom Movement's March on Liberty." Imagine that you were one of the tens of thousands of African American and white citizens who attended the August 28, 1963 March on Washington. Refer to pages 422–423 and write a paragraph describing your reaction to the event based on the bulleted items.

Compose your paragraph on separate paper.

- Explain why you marched, and what effect you hoped to have on society.

- Discuss Dr. Martin Luther King's speech and the effect it had on the marchers.

Student Traveler

List six major cities in the South in which civil rights events are described in Unit 13. Write a brief description of each event.

1. _____

2. _____

3. _____

4. _____

5. _____

6. _____

African American Cultural Themes

Working together in teams, compare and contrast the meaning of the following quotations from Unit 13:

James Lawson's statement on nonviolence, page 415

Dr. King's speech in Montgomery, Alabama, page 427

The use of the term "Black Power!" by activists Willie Ricks and Stokely Carmichael, page 432

Create two posters on the subject of love, peace, and community that you can imagine civil rights demonstrators carrying. Write an explanation of how the message on each poster reflects the African American cultural themes of humanism and/or communalism. Use the space provided to create the messages and explanations.

Create your posters on separate paper.

Unit 13 highlights all nine African American cultural themes:

- **Resilience**
- **Humanism**
- **Communalism**
- **Emotional Vitality**
- **Spirituality**
- **Realness**
- **Orality and Verbal Expressiveness**
- **Musicality/Rhythm**
- **Personal Style and Uniqueness**

Refer to page viii for a description of these themes.

The freedom movements were legendary for their highly spirited demands for equal rights. Their opponents retaliated with violence and many African Americans and white supporters were seriously hurt or killed. This called for even greater courage, determination, and faith from the African American community to continue to lead the struggle for equal rights (resilience, humanism, communalism, emotional vitality, and spirituality). The church rallies where speakers openly spoke the truth about racism and discrimination, daily demonstrations, and the singing of spirituals or freedom songs created a bond that brought people of all colors and backgrounds together to protest racism (spirituality, humanism, communalism, realness, orality and verbal expressiveness, musicality/rhythm, personal style and uniqueness, emotional vitality).

Messages	Explanations

Note-taking Tips | PREWRITING

Note cards are a good
way to organize
your writing.

You have written a new book entitled *Martin and Malcolm: Brothers in the Struggle.* The manuscript is ready for a publisher. In this activity you will prepare a one-page publishing proposal to a publishing company. (See the Center Your Writing activity on page 451 of the textbook.) Answer the questions below to help you prepare your proposal.

Note-taking Tips:

Review the sections about Malcolm X and Dr. Martin Luther King, Jr. in your textbook, particularly page 449. Include specific details in your answers.

1. Do people know about the contributions that Malcolm X and Dr. Martin Luther King, Jr. made to the struggle for civil rights? What is significant about their contributions?

   _____

   _____

   _____

   _____

   _____

Explain:

Explain why it is important for people to know about these two leaders.

2. Do people understand the reasons that Martin and Malcolm might be called brothers? What are some of these reasons?

   _____

   _____

   _____

   _____

   _____

   _____

Describe:

Choose a specific target audience. Who would benefit most from this book?

3. Is the book written for adults or children? African Americans or a diverse population? schools or the general public?

   _____

   _____

   _____

   _____

   _____

   _____

Drafting Tips	# DRAFTING

Use your notes to prepare the first draft.

Use the answers to the questions to help you draft your proposal. Remember that you must convince the publisher of the value of this book and identify potential customers who would buy it.

Publisher's address: (You may use the address in the front of your textbook.)

_____

_____

Your Address: _____

_____

Date: _____

Dear Publisher:

First Paragraph:

Begin with a general description of the book and why you think the information in it is important and relevant today.

1. Explain your reason(s) for writing the book. _____

_____

_____

Second Paragraph:

Clearly state the theme(s) of the book and include supporting details.

2. Identify the main theme(s) of the book. _____

_____

_____

Concluding Paragraph:

Identify your target audience and explain why they will want to read the book. Use the last few sentences to "sell" the book to the publisher.

3. Describe the "target audience"—the kinds of people that you believe will be interested in reading the book. _____

_____

_____

_____

_____

_____

Sincerely yours,

signature

Revising and Proofreading Tips

REVISING AND PROOFREADING

Polish and clean up your writing as you prepare for publication.

Review your proposal to determine whether it is clear and makes sense. As you read, mark the letter for improvements. Check to see whether you have included all the important information from your notes. Revise your proposal on the lines below.

Organization:

Check to make sure you have written a well-organized letter.

Edit:

Anything in your proposal that does not add to your topic and main ideas should be removed.

Sentence Length:

Use some shorter, simple sentences between complex and compound ones.

Word Choice:

Have you used the best words to convey your meaning? Focus on choosing the best possible verbs and adjectives.

Check Your Style:

Fix any sentences that are choppy or awkward.

Proofread:

Check for problems with grammar, usage, punctuation, capitalization, and spelling.

_____

_____

_____

_____

_____

_____

_____

_____

_____

_____

_____

_____

_____

_____

_____

_____

_____

_____

_____

_____

_____

_____

_____

_____

_____

_____

_____

_____

Publishing Tips

PUBLISHING

Prepare your report for publication.

Visual Appeal:

Check your finished product to make sure it is visually appealing. The format for a business letter should be followed. Consider typing the letter to make it look professional.

Copy your clean, final proposal on the lines below. With your teacher's help, decide how you want to "publish" your proposal. You may want to read it to your class, add it to your scrapbook or writing portfolio, or post it on the bulletin board for others to read.

_____
_____
_____
_____
_____
_____
_____
_____
_____
_____
_____
_____
_____
_____
_____
_____
_____
_____
_____
_____
_____
_____
_____
_____
_____

Visual Literacy

Although the title of Unit 14 is "Winning Through Law," some chapters introduce radical, militant protest. Look at the photographs on pages 448, 453, 454, and 455. What are the similarities in these photographs? What emotions do they evoke? On the lines provided, express your reaction to the photographs.

_____
_____
_____
_____
_____
_____

Historical Context

The year 1968 was one of great tragedies. Review the story of Dr. Martin Luther King Jr.'s assassination on page 443 of your textbook, and Lil' Bobby Hutton's death on pages 454–455. Read about other violent events of that year, and write an essay based on the bulleted items.

Compose your essay on separate paper.

- Identify several violent events against African Americans that marked the year.

- Discuss the reasons for the violence that rocked the nation.

- Assess the results of the violence.

Student Traveler

Several chapters in Unit 14 describe dramatic events of the 1960s. Imagine that you are a time-traveler taking a trip back to one particular day in the 1960s, to a specific location in the United States. Write your eyewitness account of an event that you believe will be significant to the future of the Civil Rights Movement.

_____
_____
_____
_____
_____
_____
_____
_____
_____
_____
_____

African American Cultural Themes

Review the chart, The Seven Principles of Kwanzaa, on page 460 of your textbook. Then conduct additional research on Malcolm X and on Kwanzaa. In teams of two, discuss the meaning of these principles and then work together to create two summaries. 1) Malcolm X: Principles of Kwanzaa in his Life. 2) The Relationships Between the Kwanzaa Principles: Umoja, Ujima, Ujamaa, and the African American Cultural Theme of Communalism. Use the concept map provided to plan your summaries.

Write your summaries on separate paper.

Many times, the study of the biographies of African American people who have made major contributions to the freedom struggle can serve as excellent references to important African American cultural principles. Unit 14 highlights all of the nine African American Cultural Themes.

- **Communalism**
- **Realness**
- **Musicality/Rhythm**
- **Orality and Verbal Expressiveness**
- **Emotional Vitality**
- **Personal Style and Uniqueness**
- **Spirituality**
- **Humanism**
- **Resilience**

Refer to page viii for a description of these themes.

Malcolm X, featured in Chapter 48, was a dynamic leader who showed by example many of the themes in traditional African American culture. His strong sense of African community was central to his life's work (communalism). He was bold and outspoken (realness) and never backed down despite the numerous death threats directed at him and his family. Malcolm's audiences were deeply moved by his intelligence and the fiery, rhythmic style he used to inform and persuade others (musicality/rhythm, orality and verbal expressiveness, emotional vitality). Malcolm was unique in many ways (personal style and uniqueness). He rose to leadership from an unlikely background in crime and converted to the Muslim faith during his term in prison. As a Muslim and activist, Malcolm was committed to the empowerment of African Americans as well as all people of color in the African diaspora (spirituality, humanism). His courage, commitment, and fierce determination uplifted others and gave them hope (resilience).

MALCOLM X

KWANZAA PRINCIPLES

COMMUNALISM

Part A
Answering Document-Based Questions

Document-Based Questions test your ability to analyze a group of documents.

Word Choice:

Focus on how the choice of words expresses the writer's attitude toward the subject. Is the tone militant, scholarly, practical, or diplomatic?

Analyze:

Data in a table or graph can be used to find out about social policies and political priorities that may favor some groups and leave others behind.

Review this unit, which discusses the new self-awareness among African Americans and their efforts to achieve a society in which everyone is treated equally.

Directions: The following questions are based on documents in Unit 15. Review each document, then answer the questions that follow.

Document #1: Analyzing a Primary Source (Page 502)
Review Maxine Waters's speech in the textbook.

1. Does the tone of Maxine Waters's speech match that of Booker T. Washington or of W. E. B. Du Bois? Explain.

_____

_____

2. List two devices that Maxine Waters uses in her speech and explain how they demonstrate the cultural themes of orality and verbal expressiveness.

_____

_____

Document #2: Analyzing a Table (Page 485)
Review the table in your textbook entitled "Total Americans Employed in Professional Fields and the Percent that are African American, 1996."

1. In which five fields are African Americans the least represented?

_____

_____

Document #3: Analyzing a Graph (Page 493)
Review the graph in your textbook entitled "African American Income in Various Categories, 1970–1995."

1. Has the percentage of African Americans earning less than $10,000 changed in this period? How does that compare to the other categories?

_____

_____

2. What problem in the African American community does this graph identify?

_____

_____

Part B
Drafting a Document-Based Essay

Drafting Tips

Review Unit 15. Take notes of supporting details that can be used in your essay.

Historical Context: While the Civil Rights Act of 1964 prohibited discrimination, further action was needed to bring about change. Affirmative action policies, though debated from the start, were established to address this need.

Task: Imagine that you have been called to testify before a committee that is investigating the need for affirmative action programs. Using the data and quotations from the three sources in Part A, write an essay that you can use to summarize your report. In your essay, discuss the following:

- Identify and explain the problem of African American earnings.

- Refer to the information in the table on occupations to identify the under-representation of African Americans in certain fields.

- Use a quote from Maxine Waters's speech to support your position.

Thesis Statement:

Write a thesis statement that identifies the topic of your essay. Be careful not to simply restate the topic.

Thesis Statement: _____

_____

_____

_____

Analysis:

Think about how your answers to the document-based questions support the thesis statement.

Analysis: _____

_____

_____

_____

Supporting Ideas:

Generate a list of details that support your thesis statement. Use a quote or other specific details from one or more of the documents to support your thesis statement.

Supporting Ideas: _____

_____

_____

_____

_____

Conclusion:

End your essay with a concluding paragraph that restates or sums up your main ideas.

Conclusion: _____

_____

_____

_____

_____

Revising and Proofreading Tips

REVISING AND PROOFREADING

Polish and clean up your writing as you prepare for publication.

Read your essay aloud to determine whether it is clear and makes sense. As you read, mark the sentences that can be improved. Check to see whether you have used all the important information from your notes. Revise your essay on the lines below.

Organization:

Check to make sure you have written a well-organized essay that includes an introduction, several supporting paragraphs, and a conclusion.

Edit:

Anything in your essay that does not add to your thesis and supporting ideas should be removed.

Sentence Length:

Use some shorter, simple sentences between complex and compound ones.

Word Choice:

Have you used the best words to convey your meaning? Focus on choosing the best possible verbs and adjectives.

Check Your Style:

Fix any sentences that are choppy or awkward.

Proofread:

Check for problems with grammar, usage, punctuation, capitalization, and spelling.

_____
_____
_____
_____
_____
_____
_____
_____
_____
_____
_____
_____
_____
_____
_____
_____
_____
_____
_____
_____
_____
_____
_____
_____
_____
_____
_____
_____

Publishing Tips

Prepare your essay for publication.

Visual Appeal:

Check your finished product to make sure it is visually appealing. The margins should be uniform and the lines evenly spaced. If you want to post your essay, it should be written in clear, bold letters. Use a dark ink pen, rather than pencil or red pen. Make sure the title is in large print so that it stands out.

Adding Graphics:

Consider adding a graphic—such as a photograph, an illustration, or a map—to enhance the "look" of your final product and further support your ideas.

PUBLISHING

Copy the clean, final version of your essay on the lines below and add a title. With your teacher's help, decide how you want to "publish" your essay. You may want to post it on the classroom bulletin board, make a class scrapbook or writing portfolio, or read it to the class.

_____

_____

_____

_____

_____

_____

_____

_____

_____

_____

_____

_____

_____

_____

_____

_____

_____

_____

_____

_____

_____

_____

_____

_____

_____

_____

Visual Literacy

In Unit 15 there are many photographs of noted African Americans and Africans. Scan the unit to find those who are wearing clothing that represents African, not western, culture. Name the individuals and describe the differences in the appearance of western and African clothing.

1. Individuals: _____

_____

_____

_____

2. Description of differences: _____

_____

_____

_____

_____

Historical Context

Choose an artist from the Black Arts Movement in Chapter 51. Research the person and his or her art and write a short essay based on the bulleted items.

Compose your essay on separate paper.

- Describe the life of the chosen artist.
- Identify his or her art and the importance of this person's contributions to the Black Arts Movement.

Student Traveler

Chapter 52 contains a map of Black Studies Programs at universities in the United States. Take a virtual tour of one of these universities and investigate its graduate program in Black Studies. Begin your tour on the university's web site (UCLA.edu, Cornell.edu etc. Your library will have the Internet addresses.) List the course offerings in the space provided.

_____

_____

_____

_____

_____

_____

_____

_____

_____

_____

_____

African American Cultural Themes

Imagine that you are a group of students studying filmmaking. Your assignment is to make a short film clip about the events in Unit 15. First you must create a storyboard consisting of 10 large panels or boxes. Each panel includes a sketch of one of the main scenes that will be in the movie and a written description of the people, setting, and action for that scene. In addition, your storyboard description includes a reference to the cultural themes that are demonstrated in that scene. When completed, present your storyboard to the class.

On the lines provided, write one or two sentences describing each of the 10 scenes from your storyboard.

You may use the blank pages at the back of the Worktext if you need additional space.

The revolutionary climate of the late 1960s sparked a new self-awareness in African American culture that was reflected in the Black Arts Movement. Unit 15 highlights eight of the nine African American cultural themes:

- **Emotional Vitality**
- **Musicality/Rhythm**
- **Orality and Verbal Expressiveness**
- **Realness**
- **Personal Style and Uniqueness**
- **Resilience**
- **Humanism**
- **Communalism**

Refer to page viii for a description of these themes.

In the opening chapter of this unit, the author provides examples of African Americans' energetic, creative outpourings in the arts (emotional vitality, musicality and rhythm, orality and verbal expressiveness, realness, personal style and uniqueness). The Black Arts Movement was highly cultural and directly reflected the political, racial, and social upheavals of the times. In the remaining chapters, you read how the determination and unrelenting creative energy of African Americans working together (resilience) resulted in the demand for the establishment of Black Studies, affirmative action, and a just and fair society (humanism, communalism).

_____

_____

_____

_____

_____

_____

_____

_____

_____

_____

_____

_____

_____

Note-taking Tips | PREWRITING

Note-taking Tips

Answer all the questions to develop a comprehensive theme on cultural traditions.

Research:

Find out more about your cultural heritage by talking to family members and friends.

Reflect:

Are you involved in a club, religious tradition, or cultural organization that allows you to learn more about your heritage? If so, what have you learned?

Discuss:

Talk to your parents, grandparents, or other adults about cultural traditions that are important to pass along to future generations.

Think:

Have you ever attended a festival or other type of special event that taught you more about another cultural tradition? Think about how this has affected you.

Dr. Asante writes that America is a "vibrant mixture of cultural diversity in one unified nation." In this writing assignment you will create a personal journal of your cultural journey toward this ideal. This activity will help you assess your own cultural traditions and your hopes and dreams for America's future. Answer the following questions as you prepare to write a personal journal of your cultural journey.

1. What cultural traditions have you learned from your parents, grandparents, or extended family?

   _____

   _____

2. How have you shared your culture with people of other cultures?

   _____

   _____

3. What motivates you to want to share your culture?

   _____

   _____

4. Why is it important to keep cultural traditions alive?

   _____

   _____

5. What steps have you taken to learn more about the cultural traditions of others?

   _____

   _____

6. What will you do to help pass on your cultural traditions to future generations?

   _____

   _____

7. What are your hopes and dreams for the future of cultural diversity and ethnic unity in the United States and the world?

   _____

   _____

Drafting Tips	**DRAFTING**

Use your notes to prepare your first draft.

Use your responses from the Prewriting activity to plan a personal journal about your cultural journey. Remember to use enough interesting and informative details about your cultural traditions, and your feelings about those traditions, to learn more about yourself and your heritage.

Introduction:

Begin the journal by discussing your feelings about personal cultural traditions.

Introduction: _____

_____

_____

_____

_____

_____

_____

Supporting Paragraphs:

Include your responses to the Prewriting questions in a logical order that builds on your theme about cultural traditions and diversity. You may want to combine more than one response into a single paragraph.

Supporting Paragraphs: _____

_____

_____

_____

_____

_____

_____

_____

_____

_____

_____

_____

Conclusion:

End your essay with a description of your hopes and dreams for ethnic unity and cultural diversity.

Conclusion: _____

_____

_____

_____

_____

_____

Revising and Proofreading Tips

REVISING AND PROOFREADING

Polish and clean up your writing as you prepare for publication.

The information used in your personal journal should support the main idea—an exploration of your cultural identity.

MY CULTURAL JOURNEY

First Person:

Write in the first person as you describe the cultural traditions you want to preserve.

Personal Voice:

Use your "personal voice" to convey your opinions and experiences.

Sentence Length:

Use some shorter, simple sentences between complex and compound ones.

Word Choice:

Have you used the best words to convey your meaning? Focus on choosing the best possible verbs and adjectives.

Proofread:

Check for problems with grammar, usage, punctuation, capitalization, and spelling.

Publishing Tips | PUBLISHING

Prepare the final version of your personal journal.

Copy the clean final version of your journal on the lines below.

MY CULTURAL JOURNEY

Visual Appeal:

Check your finished product to make sure it is visually appealing. The margins should be uniform and the lines evenly spaced. If you want to share your journal with others, it should be written in clear, bold letters. Use a dark ink pen, rather than pencil or red pen.

Adding Graphics:

Consider adding a graphic—such as a photograph, an illustration, or a map—to enhance the "look" of your final product.

Visual Literacy

On the Unit 16 Opener pages, observe the collage of some African Americans who have made significant contributions to modern American history and culture. The contributions of many of these outstanding individuals were discussed in this unit. Write a caption that links the collage to the quote by Mari Evans at the top of the page. On separate paper, write the name and accomplishments of each person.

Caption: _____

_____

_____

_____

_____

_____

Historical Context

Each year, the Museum of African American History in Detroit honors an outstanding African American who has made an historic contribution to the advancement of African American history and culture. Using information from the textbook and photos and captions in the New Horizons color visuals on page C7, write a nominating letter to the museum's selection committee.

Compose your letter on separate paper.

- Recommend a contemporary African American worthy of this honor.

- State the nominee's accomplishments.

- Explain why this person is uniquely qualified to join the other prominent African Americans whose names are displayed on the rotunda floor of the museum.

Student Traveler

African Americans continue to make notable contributions to the political life of the United States. Use your textbook and other resources to research data on African American mayors, governors, and members of Congress (House and Senate) from 1966 to the present. Then create a map from your research. Use the map to answer the following questions.

1. Which large cities have elected African Americans as mayors?

_____

2. Which states have elected African Americans as governors?

_____

3. Who are the African Americans currently serving as mayors and governors? _____

_____

4. Who are the African Americans currently serving as members of Congress? _____

_____

African American Cultural Themes

Chapter 57 opens with a quote from author Richard Wright, who declared: "African American people are America's metaphor for hope."

Working with a partner, conduct additional research to find ten noted African Americans in the arts, literature, education, entertainment, business, law, space, sports, and philosophy. Select one person from your list that you most admire and who gives you hope for the future. In the space provided, create a 60-second public service announcement that describes the reasons for your admiration. Prepare to share it in written and oral form.

Unit 16 describes the achievements of African Americans in many different fields. Their accomplishments highlight eight of the nine African American cultural themes:

- Spirituality
- Musicality/Rhythm
- Orality and Verbal Expressiveness
- Personal Style and Uniqueness
- Emotional Vitality
- Communalism
- Resilience
- Humanism

Refer to page viii for a description of these themes.

Wright's message illuminates the African American journey to liberation. He makes it clear that despite enslavement, oppressive racism, and discrimination, African Americans have persisted, endured, and continued to work together to make grand and original contributions to our great nation (spirituality, musicality/rhythm, orality and verbal expressiveness, personal style and uniqueness, emotional vitality, communalism, resilience, humanism). In doing so, African Americans have given hope to all oppressed peoples regardless of their economic background, race, religion, or nationality.

Name _____

Date _____

Assignment _____

Name _____

Date _____

Assignment _____

Name _____

Date _____

Assignment _____

Name _____

Date _____

Assignment _____